"Jen's encouragement to j[...]
tion and to live while dying is inspiring.

HOLLYE JACOBS
RN, MS, MSW

"Jen Smith is one of those AMAZING people who cares SO MUCH about sharing her story—the good and the bad—to help and empower others in the fight!! She always keeps a positive attitude, and she is a TRUE INSPIRATION to everyone out there touched by cancer! Our team loves her—DEARLY!!!!"

JONNY IMERMAN
Founder, Imerman Angels 1-on-1 Cancer Support

"We need more women like Jen Smith to educate us about the realities of living with metastatic breast cancer at a young age."

JODY SCHOGER
Breast Cancer Survivor, Advocate, and Writer

"Exiled to Cancerland, Jen Smith is a brave and reliable guide through tough, heartbreaking terrain."

JOANNA CHAPMAN
Author of *Divine Secrets of the Ta-Ta Sisterhood: Pledging the Pink Sorority*

WHAT YOU MIGHT NOT KNOW

Cover and interior design by Parkland College Typography II class, Spring 2013

Author picture by Allyson Sanborn, Sweet Pea Photography
Author picture by Teri Fuller

Printed in the United States of America

First Printing, 2013
ISBN 978-1-300-73004-0
ISBN e book 978-1-300-96586-2

Jennifer Smith
Champaign, IL

www.livinglegendary.org

WHAT
YOU MIGHT
NOT KNOW

My Life as a Stage IV Cancer Patient

JENNIFER SMITH
with Teri Fuller

TABLE OF CONTENTS

A VERY BRIEF YET HEARTFELT FOREWORD

Unlike some other cancer memoirs that are all-to-polished and clever, *What You Might Not Know: My Life as a Stage IV Cancer Patient* tells us what it is really like. For most of us, attempting to understand this is like trying to enter a door that has neither lock nor key. We know someone who is on the other side, and we can hear their words and even sense some of their movements, but we are unable to cross the threshold. That is why this book is so very important: It allows us to get to the other side, so that we may no longer have to look on helplessly—from afar—as our friend, partner, relative, or patient makes sense of a metastatic diagnosis.

Because her words are far more important than mine, I have kept this foreword brief, so that you may now turn the page and get to that other side.

Teri Fuller,
Breast Cancer Patient, Advocate, and Writer

PREFACE

I was diagnosed with breast cancer when I was thirty years old. I endured a lumpectomy, a grueling six months of chemotherapy, and seven weeks of daily radiation. Just three months after treatment was over, the scans showed the cancer was back. There was a recurrence in my breast and multiple tumors in my bones. I was thirty-one when I was diagnosed with Stage IV breast cancer, which meant the cancer had spread to other parts of my body. This diagnosis is incurable and terminal.

Since my Stage IV diagnosis, I have tried to shield others from my reality—especially my son, whom I love most dearly. When others asked how I was doing, I oftentimes said, "I'm fine." The truth, though, is that I wasn't fine, and others deserved to know the truth. That is why I decided to write this book—to let others know what it's like to live each day with my own murderer: Stage IV breast cancer.

Writing, though, hasn't been easy. I am trained as a counselor, so I'm used to being the one to comfort others; opening up is a role reversal for me. But I know there is so much power in exposing the truth, especially when it's pure and authentic.

In addition to sharing my own perspective, I've also included the views and feelings of my close friends and family who have also been affected by this disease. These are the people who have gotten me through. Their perspectives and sentiments are crucial in telling the whole story.

At the end of the book, I included "Jen's Top Ten" and listed cancer-related charities that do not have million dollar marketing budgets. If you are able, I'd be ever-grateful for a donation to any of them.

I invite you into my story in the hopes that I can share a glimpse of the reality of Stage IV breast cancer. Welcome to the other side of the pink ribbon where the truth of metastatic disease is exposed.

Jen

"Writing is a form of *therapy*; sometimes I wonder how all those who do not write, compose or paint can manage to escape the madness, melancholia, the panic and *fear* which is inherent in a human situation."

Graham Greene

WRITING

I was determined to process this very madness, melancholia, panic, and fear after one of my close friends died of metastatic breast cancer, or cancer that had spread to her vital organs including her bones, liver, and lungs. This is the same type of cancer I was diagnosed with more than four years ago. A metastatic, or Stage IV, breast cancer diagnosis is considered incurable and terminal and has an average life expectancy of less than three years. The product of this endeavor was my first memoir, *Learning to Live Legendary*.

I initially met my friend, Erin, by way of an online message board for young women diagnosed with breast cancer. We connected because we understood each other; we were both diagnosed with metastatic breast cancer during the fall of 2008 at age 31. At first, we corresponded through the online message board, but then we became more intimate and began to exchange emails as well as text messages. We integrated ourselves into each other's lives quite effortlessly because our biographies were so similar.

A year after finding one another on this message board, Erin and I finally met in person at the Conference for Young Women with breast cancer in Atlanta, Georgia, in February 2010. Sometimes meeting someone in person isn't as satisfying as one would hope, but meeting Erin was even more gratifying than I could have visualized. I remember meeting her in the lobby, seeing her spectacular smile as she walked up and hugged me big and long. Although her hair was blonde and mine was brown, we both had a short pixie cut as our hair was growing back after chemotherapy. Erin and I were the same height, 5'11", and we joked about being the Amazonian breast cancer twins at the conference. We also both worked at community colleges; she with career advising, I with academic advising. We talked about our divorces; mine more recent, hers years in the past. She gave me hope about romantic relationships, though, as she told me about her devoted fiancé who continued to love her even more profoundly after her diagnosis. We attended research and educational sessions together at the conference and dressed in our favorite little black dresses one evening, joining several hundred other young survivors who danced until the DJ stopped at midnight—even though the young survivors could have danced well into the morning hours.

Our unique friendship intensified after we connected in person at the conference. As this happened, I saw how Erin really lived after and during a terminal diagnosis. Shortly after the young survivor's conference in Atlanta, Erin appeared on Season 5 of TLC's hit show *Say Yes to the Dress*, which documented her search for the perfect wedding gown at the premiere bridal salon Klienfeld's in New York City. In one scene, Erin found *the* dress, but it also had a five-figure price tag. It was a beautiful white Carolina Herrera gown with an elegant fawn-colored sash and bow. Erin commented that she was self-conscious about her port and scar showing just below her collarbone. While a port is vital to infuse chemotherapy, it isn't something she wanted visible in her wedding photographs. The assistant at Klienfeld's suggested they add some extra ruffles to the straps to conceal the port. Hiding the port and scar wasn't the only problem though. Her hair was falling out from chemotherapy, so she added a partial wig and vintage tiara to conceal the side effects of treatment. The final look was flawless. The staff at Klienfeld's sympathized with Erin's story and worked to get the dress in her budget. Having found the perfect dress, she traveled to Spain, where her future mother-in-law lived. There she married a partner who deeply and bravely loved her. I can still remember her telling me the details of her wedding day—how she and her new husband took a myriad of pictures throughout small villages in Spain. With the life she still had, she chose to live—not die.

When Erin returned from her wedding, we got together in Cleveland, Ohio. One evening we met up with one of my friends from college and a few of her girlfriends. That summer night we dined outside at LaStrada, enjoying Italian food and fine wine. As we were getting to know one another, one of the girls asked Erin what she did for a living. She boldly said, "My job is to be healthy. I get massages, go to yoga, juice, stay up-to-date on research, and stay away from stress." I remember Erin confidently telling others about her "job."

I also remember the Conference for Young Women with breast cancer the following year, which was held in Orlando, Florida—where Erin lived with Adam. She offered to pick me and three other Stage IV roommates up at the airport. Although Tracy, Marcia, Shayne, and I needed to stay at the hotel for the conference, Erin became our unofficial roommate. She generously served as our private driver in Orlando, and while doing so, she told us much about her life there. Since Erin was local, she was our honorary roommate at the prominent Peabody Hotel, hanging out in our room before and after sessions, but going home to her husband at night. I remember one night we walked to Taverna Opa, Erin's favorite Greek restaurant. While we waited for a table, we sat on a fountain outside the restaurant and asked a passer-by to take a picture of the five of us. I imagine the stranger had no idea that the five of us, all under 40, were living with a murderer, Stage IV breast cancer. Once we were seated at our table, the restaurant seemed designed to excite every sense. The atmosphere was like a college frat party with staff and diners dancing on the tables. Greek music filled the air, and everyone was clapping, laughing, or dancing along. The aroma of traditional Greek roasted lamb succulently wafted through the restaurant. Not only was Taverna Opa a wonderful place to eat, it was also a wonderful place for entertainment. Erin had danced on the tables previously and encouraged me to do the same; however, I had a severe radiation burn down the back of my leg, making it difficult to walk, let alone dance. Turning down that opportunity with her is still one of my greatest regrets in life.

But it wasn't just in these monumental moments that she evidenced her drive to really live—it was also in the very thoughtful exchanges we had before, during, and after our visit in Orlando. Erin wasn't just about living for herself; she also lived for others, and I was fortunate enough to be one of those others. She would often ask how I was doing, even though her own disease was progressing; she was the one in more immediate need. She also connected with newly-diagnosed women on the online breast cancer boards and articulated ways to keep living, despite having a terminal diagnosis. Her desire to live was evident in the big and the small, in the public and the private, and all the while in the in-between.

Even though I knew that Erin's cancer continued to spread, prompting a spine surgery in September 2011, I never expected she would become so gravely ill so quickly. The goal of the surgery was to alleviate the intense pain caused by a cancer-ridden vertebra that was collapsing and pinching nerves. Although Erin lived in Orlando with her husband, she chose to have the surgery at the renowned Cleveland Clinic which was close to her parent's home. She got through the arduous surgery and began recovering at her parents. The goal was to have the pain under control and continue with treatment to try and stabilize the disease throughout her body. On Monday, October 17, 2011, my phone rang. It was Tracy, who had been one of our Stage IV roommates at the conference in Orlando. Tracy sounded nervous and asked if she was interrupting anything. I explained that I was at home cleaning and had time to chat. Tracy's worried tone came tumbling out in words, "Erin was admitted to the hospital in the middle of the night and doesn't have long." I gasped for a breath; my heart throbbed as tears poured down my face. "Ok," I said, "I'm throwing a few things in a suitcase and getting on the road." I packed with both urgency and dread. I made phone calls to arrange child care for my son. I tried to be stoic as I told my mom that I was rushing to say good-bye to Erin. I was outraged that the disease had devoured her body, and her impending death was an unexpected shock. I felt desperate to connect with her again. And I could not conceive of what my life would be like without Erin.

What, after all, was happening? I had just spoken with Erin the week before and had no way of knowing her health would rapidly deteriorate in several days. I knew from Tracy's call that she didn't have long, and I had an eight-hour drive to get to Cleveland. I drove from Illinois to Ohio in a whirling-dervish of a fury, stopping only once to refuel. As I drove, I thought only of her—how she loved her cats, named after fashion icons Ralph (Lauren), Louie (Louis Vuitton), and Hugo (Boss). I remembered her love for Lady Gaga's music and fashion designer Tory Burch. I thought of her fervent love story with her husband. And all the while, I panicked at the thought of her death. I wondered: Is this what my death would be like? Would others feel this same panic when I was dying?

I arrived at Hillcrest Hospital and ran to the Intensive Care Unit. I asked for Erin's room, and the nurse paused. I could smell the hospital sterility. I could hear machines beeping, tracking heart rates and breathing. And, in that pause, it was then I knew. I was too late; Erin had already died.

Erin's mom appeared in the hallway, and even though we'd never met, she simply said, "Oh, Jen; you're here." She hugged me long and hard, just like Erin had when we originally met. She took me back to Erin's room. There, Erin's body was still connected to medical tubing and wires, but the machines were still. Erin looked peaceful, lying in the hospital bed. Her father stood solemnly in the corner, staring at his daughter. Her husband sat on the edge of her bed, rubbing her arm and still talking to her, comforting her: Telling her she was beautiful; telling her that he loved her; telling her she was strong, brave, and now at peace. Erin's mom wept as she showed the nurses Erin's wedding pictures and told of her fairytale romance. It was as if those pictures showed the "healthy" Erin that her mother desperately wanted back.

I was in shock and felt numb. Her bereaved husband looked at me and said, "You get this, Jen, more than any of us here do. Any of us could get hit by a bus tomorrow, but we don't see the bus today, knowing that is our fate. We aren't reminded of our own mortality each and every time we see a bus." After several moments of silence, I said my goodbye to Erin and kissed her on the cheek. I thanked the family as they let me have a final goodbye and some sense of closure. I returned to the main hallway, empty that night, and saw Tracy. We embraced for a lengthy hug, as tears poured down our faces, and then we sat on a bench, openly crying and mourning the loss of Erin.

With Erin's death being so unexpected, it took several days to arrange her funeral. I realized that staying for the funeral wasn't possible because I had a chemotherapy session back in Illinois, that I couldn't reschedule. During the drive home from Cleveland in mid-October, I didn't see the brilliant fall colors of the foliage. Instead I found that the landscape resembled a bleak winter day that mirrored my emotions. Rain poured down during the eight-hour drive home. Winds gusted and nearly took my car off the road after passing a semi. Visibility barely extended beyond the front hood of my car.

The storm that rained down outside of the car seemed to seep in as well. Words came to me—words that I would later write down—words that would help me to understand and heal. The words at first were as sad and wet as the rain crashing down on my car, but then the words became lighter and formed images in my mind of the healthy Erin—the one who lived life with love and light.

When I finally returned to the cornfields of Illinois, I saw the farmers harvesting their grain. And while they were reaping what they had sown, I began to plant the first linguistic seeds that came to me. I put words down on paper, and these words were the ones that helped me process.

I knew I couldn't engage in this arduous writing process alone. After all, I was not trained as a writer. So I contacted a friend who knew about both breast cancer and writing. She was my age and diagnosed just three months after me when her daughter was only 9-months old. My son, Corbin, was only 10-months old when I was diagnosed; our children were just a few months apart in age. Besides being a cancer survivor and advocate, Teri Fuller is also a writing professor in Chicago. She was my perfect writing companion, so I asked her if she would be willing to edit and infuse her brilliance into my story. Thankfully she agreed, and I started writing. And while it was therapeutic, it was also entirely exhausting. In doing so, I spent many hours writing, editing, and revising. At first, I wasn't sure what my exact purpose was, but in the end, my first memoir became a "thank you" to all the people who had helped me to *truly live*—just as my friend Erin had done—despite having a terminal diagnosis. I remember how I had made a bucket list in 2011 of dozens of items, ranging from traveling to a place I'd never been to simply dancing on a bar. Now, looking back at my list after Erin's death, I regret not getting on the table and dancing with her. In addition to thanking my audience—the people who allowed me to fulfill my bucket list—I wanted my readers to understand why I had chosen each item on my list—why each item was monumental. I wanted my audience to understand that it is possible to live—even while dying.

That was my first book: A thank you to those who helped me really *live*. This, though, is my second, and I aim to privately process all that I've experienced while simultaneously and publicly writing, articulating, and revealing the authentic realities of metastatic breast cancer. Various writers have said that to write, you have to open up a vein and bleed, and for me, that's what writing this book has felt like as I have exposed the raw reality of living with Stage IV breast cancer. I want people who don't have the disease to better understand it, so they can empathize with and uplift people in their own lives who are also struggling. And most importantly, I want these words to insist that everyone really experience the human condition and *live*—even while dying.

"My metastatic *cancer* diagnosis doesn't just affect me: it affects the people who *care* about and for me."

REFLECTING

MY metastatic cancer diagnosis doesn't just affect me: it affects the people who care about and for me. In addition to my family, my close friends have supported me. Here are their feelings.

This is Jill, my college roommate:

> There are those major moments in your life when time seems to stop and the rest of the world fades into a blur. These *big* life-changing moments come into my life in the form of two simple words.
>
> In 1997, my little brother was in a terrible car accident. He lay lifeless in ICU for a week, and on July 27th, 1997 my grandfather walked into our house and opened his arms to take me in them, tears running down his face and said: *He's gone.*
>
> On October 23rd, 2004, I stood at the altar at St. James Church and declaring before God, my friends, family, and my soon-to-be husband: *I do.*

At 4:26pm on October 24th, 2006, after 10 hours of exhausting labor, the doctor looked up at me holding my brand new beautiful baby girl and said: *She's here.*

On September 7th, 2007, walking down the hallway at my parents' house, getting ready for a dinner date, I looked down at my phone at an incoming text message from my college roommate, and it said: *It's cancer.*

It's cancer.

It's quite amazing two simple words can bring you to your knees, take your breath away, and change your life. I literally put my hand over my mouth and just stared wide-eyed at the screen, thinking if I stare long enough a "NOT" will magically appear between "it's" and "cancer." Well, that "not" I was searching for didn't ever appear. Instead the word CANCER seemed to get larger and larger the more I stared at it. The words had to be a mistake; it was impossible—she's too young, too beautiful, too healthy. Those thoughts came before the many tears. I remember thinking this can't happen to Jen. Jen was a planner; she had everything in her life organized into neat little folders and this kind of thing just doesn't happen to a young, healthy, beautiful, happy new mom. *A new mom.* She had endured so much to get pregnant with Corbin, and he was the miracle baby she was dreaming of after the heartbreaking miscarriage, frustrating doctor's appointments, and continuous disappointments.

I was there the day she went into labor. I was proudly introducing a very pregnant Jen to my week-old daughter. I actually told her, laughing at her evident yet exciting discomfort, "Oh yeah, Roomie.

I think you are in labor," since I could remember having those labor pains just a week prior. Our children, Addison and Corbin, were born just nine days apart.

My college roommate and I had been through so many things together, and even when we got mad at each other, the mutual nickname we call each other to this day, "Roomies," we'll always be. I stayed with her for a while as she worked through some early contractions, then waited with baited breath to hear Corbin had made it here safe and sound. Jen was the happiest I had ever seen her. I came to visit just two weeks after he was born, and as we sat there completely exhausted holding our newborns, there was a sense of calm in the midst of our new baby chaos. It was one of the last times I can remember that certain smile. That tired, calm, genuine, all-is-right-in-my-world smile.

Fast forward 10 short months later to September 7th. I can remember what I was wearing, I can remember where I was standing, and I can remember the old Blackberry cell phone I had. The words came at me in such an average way via a chime of a simple text message. But when I play the memory back in my mind, it now seems as if it had been in black and white, slow motion, and that chime sounds more like an eerie slow clang from a giant clock tower. I remember standing there, realizing I was standing in the same spot in my parents' home where I had been when I spoke to my little brother for the last time. That spot in the hallway holds both one of my best and worst memories.

I thought that nothing could be more painful than losing my brother. But the reality of watching my dear friend with her head in the sink crying so hard she was shaking, the tears coming from a place of sheer fear, pain, betrayal, and hurt may balance the scales. I think going through the quick death of my brother and the lingering fear I have watching one of my best friends succumb to Stage IV cancer are quite conflicting. It's like that horrible game where you get two choices and both are awful, but you have to choose one. Would you (a) chose to lose someone you love instantly, where they didn't know it was coming and they never suffered, but there was no good-bye to prepare you, or (b) would you rather watch them struggle, knowing their fate was sealed in an envelope labeled cancer? Both options are too painful to even spend more than two seconds thinking about before my brain shuts it out.

It's that age old question of would you want to know you are dying and how? My answer was always no. It's terrifying to think of death and dying. It's a terrible fear we all have as humans because we are too concerned with just . . . living. When you don't have cancer you don't think about life on a day-by-day—I'm here and living and healthy—basis. We don't have days when we say, "Oh it's a good day. I didn't feel flu-ish today." When you don't have cancer, you don't label your day as good or bad days from chemo, test results, doctor's visits, another friend dying from the same thing you are living with. I think people who are "healthy" live with rose-colored glasses on at all times.

We take so many things for granted—like my daughter going to kindergarten. It was a very happy moment for me, but in the big scheme of things, it was truly just another day. I remember sitting with Jen one night after she was diagnosed Stage IV, and she was crying because she didn't think she would see Corbin's first day of kindergarten. I sat there mystified thinking that three years from now seemed forever far away and I hadn't even begun thinking about Addison going to school. I was thinking about how I could get her to sleep without a pacifier. It was an eye-opening moment for me. Jen was living with short-term goals . . . to just get from point A to point B. And point B seemed beyond reach. Miraculously, Jen did make it to point B. The night before our kids' first day of kinder-garten, I cried, but not because I was having any feelings about Ad-dison going to "big girl school." I was thinking "*WOW*. Jen didn't even believe she would be alive tomorrow." That is *profound*. When I texted her the next morning saying I was thinking of her on this big day, she was ecstatic. She had a photographer come over and document the momentous morning. Meanwhile, I made breakfast, and my mom and I drove Addison to school, took a couple of pic-tures with my cell phone, and then I went to work. But throughout the day, dark questions arose in my mind. What if I had Stage IV cancer? It haunted me thinking of Addison not having me in her life. How would I handle knowing I wouldn't be there for all of the monumental events of her life? I take advantage of just lying on the couch with her, watching a boring kids' movie, but if I knew it would be the last movie we watched together, wouldn't I cherish every single minute? Or would I cry and ruin our time together because the reality of the cancer beast is taking any future moments from me? Because of Jen's reality, I am trying to no longer take any moment—big or small—for granted.

So many things stop me in my tracks and make me reevaluate my life. I was trying on swimsuits for our Florida vacation and I asked Addison, "Does this look OK?" She responded, "I don't like the bottom, but I like the top." The *top*. My thoughts went right to Jen. How can I complain about a swimsuit and if a certain ruffle may be unflattering when my friend doesn't even have breasts to fill a top? In a world where plastic surgery and perfection seem to be the ultimate goals for many women, how different their vanity would be if those breasts were taking their life. Are wrinkles really that bad? Wrinkles signify age, and age is a gift. A bad hair day? This one is something I laugh off these days. Jen went from beautiful blond highlights to completely bald. We went shopping one day for hats and wigs and ended up at this ridiculous wig shop run by this crass, blunt, Chicago lady. We both sat down and looked in the mirror. There we were . . . sitting in a wig shop! We weren't getting some expensive designer extensions, my friend was sitting here because in the next month she would be losing all her hair. The woman started bringing wigs for us to try on, and we were laughing at the whole situation. Finally she brought out this hideous dark, shag-cut wig, and as she was handing it to Jen, she simply stated, "Whatcha got?" My mouth hit the floor, and Jen looked up at her through the mirror and responded in the same blunt tone, "I *got* breast cancer." Hearing those words, sitting in a bad wig shop I'd had enough. When the wig shopping going gets tough, the tough get going to Nordstrom. We had a blast trying on all these beautiful, flattering hats. I told the cashier to box them up. It was the least I could do to treat her to a little hat shopping spree. It's one of my favorite pictures of us to this day. Standing there in Nordstrom, both of us in hats and smiling like, "Let's do this!"

There is so much guilt associated with being a friend of a person living with cancer. You want to spread the joy of all these things that are going so great in your life because you are friends and that is what friends do, but you ultimately hold back. I actually feared the conversation if I ever got pregnant again and how I would tell her. Jen can't have more kids. She had her ovaries removed and began menopause at the age of 31. Would it hurt her that her friends are having babies left and right with no problems when she could never experience that again? Big-time guilt. What if I got a promotion at work? Would she feel a sense of sadness because she was so successful in her career but had to quit her job because she had to accept a new position as a full-time cancer patient? Big-time guilt. What if my husband and I wanted to renew our vows? Would she feel a sense of disappointment after experiencing betrayal in her marriage that led to divorce? Big-time guilt.

But Jen wouldn't be sad, disappointed, or unhappy for any of us at all for anything. She lives her life for her friends, family, and Corbin, and to also help others who are struggling with their own diagnoses. She is an inspiration to so many people and has turned a sad, heartbreaking story into living so legendary you actually believe the saying, "If you put your mind to it and *BELIEVE*, you can accomplish anything." She puts us all at ease with the way she humbly jokes or makes light of the things cancer has taken from her. But at the same time, gives a real account of the truth that is cancer. It's a fine line, and only someone like Jen could balance both sides so gracefully.

Jen has had cancer basically the entire life span of our kids' lives. My six-year-old always refers to Jen as "the one who is sick." She doesn't know better, and it's really hard to explain to her, "Well she's not sick; she has cancer." Cancer stole both of Addison's grandparents before her birth, so I will go with sick for now. Jen came to spend the night once and she had a scarf around her bald head. She asked me if she could talk to Addie about it. It was a moment she probably doesn't even remember, but it is burned into my memory. She took off her scarf, and Addison's questions started flying. She even showed her the magic button (her port) where she gets her magic medicine (chemotherapy). The greatest moment was when Addison told her how beautiful she was even without the scarf. Then I took the most precious picture of Jen reading her a bedtime story. Addison got to see how "beautiful" someone with cancer can be, and Jen was so great explaining it to her in a way so she wouldn't be afraid.

My biggest fear is simply losing her. Losing my friend who I can count on for anything, at any time. But it's like she is indestructible—like some cancer superhero who can do it all. It just doesn't register with me she could actually *die*. I mean, we all are going to die, I know that, but it seems Jen keeps setting these goals and attaining every single one. But the word death seems to linger around our conversations, even though I like to pretend that it's not going to happen. I now fear that my mom will get cancer, that I will, or even that my daughter will. If it could happen to Jen, it could happen to any of us. She has taught me to look fear in the face and accept it. Jen doesn't like when people say she is strong or brave. I like to say she is a warrior and courageous. I read a quote that said, "Courage doesn't mean you aren't afraid. It means you are able to look that fear straight on and walk into it." Being friends with Jen has taught me many things in life, cliché as they may be: Don't sweat the small stuff, take every moment and live in it, and look fear straight on and walk into it. And I'll walk into anything and anywhere for her. I walked by her all sixty miles as we completed The 3-Day. Walking with her has forced me to walk straight into the fear of death, and I won't leave her side now.

Christie is a friend with whom I talk with weekly on the phone:

Shock hit me first, wondering; "Is this really happening to someone who is my age?" My second thought was immediately about Corbin. Third thought: Don't lose it emotionally . . .think rationally and ask, "How I can be there for you, pray for you, and give you the strength to support you?" Through that first year, I was so proud of Jen and all that she was doing to get out there and educate others. I was proud to see her as such a testimony to others, and I began to see God working through her for others. Looking back, I was kind of in denial; I felt assured she was going to beat this thing. She was so busy with all her treatment and events and raising awareness that I sat back, admiring all she was doing. Although it's hard to say this now, I sometimes felt a little jealous when I looked at myself and wondered if I would be as strong as she was in such a situation.

Then the worst day hit when I heard it was Stage IV. I just remember crying and feeling quite helpless—questioning if this praying thing really is helping. I wanted to be there more for her to help her more. And over the years seeing her continue on in treatment, I kept thinking to myself, "I don't think I could be as strong and brave as she is every day—especially with all she was dealing with aside from cancer." I took a hard look at myself and asked myself if I would do the same. Would I live to help others in this same situation? I realized how much I have missed out on actual friendships with family and friends. I then started reevaluating relationships and how very important they are to me. It was then I asked myself: "If I had a limited time on this earth, what would I do with it?"

I am still here on this earth. Why? One lesson I've learned is to cherish every person in my life. Cherish them more than anything. Make time for them; call and tell them how much you love them. Remove the impersonal things in your life. Focus on people. Spend time with the people who are important to you, and make it count. People matter; focus on them, and listen to them. Put away technology and shift focus to others to make them feel important. Be there and listen; don't waste any time on stuff that doesn't matter anymore. Tell all that you love them. God placed me here on this earth to be a person who cares and loves. Now it is my job to make every moment count—not only with my friends, but also with my family, and most of all, my children.

Linda, is my former boss whom I worked with daily at Parkland College:

My dad was one of five kids, and there were 17 cousins on that side of the family. My immediate family lived in the Columbus area, but when we were young, the rest of the family lived up near Lake Erie, where my father grew up. I sometimes wonder how we all gathered at my grandmother's house, which was nothing palatial, but we did, and you can imagine the wild fun we had with that many cousins together in close quarters. A few of the cousins were born in the 1940s, so they were the cool teenagers, while the rest of us were still in various stages of childhood awkwardness. A whole slew of cousins arrived throughout the 1950s, and the baby cousins were born in the very early 1960s.

Three of the 1950s cousins were the children of my dad's younger brother. I have some memories of him, but what I know about him I know mostly from others—that he was gentle and serious, gifted in the field of mathematics, and died shortly before his 29th birthday of Hodgkins disease, which at the time lacked the more effective treatments we have today. So in some ways, at age five, before I was old enough to understand death and its permanence, I knew that cancer could kill loved ones who are not even old.

My mom's parents lived in Oklahoma when I was a child, and we saw them rarely. Interstate highways weren't as developed as they are now, and it took two long days of driving to visit them. In December of the year I was in 8th grade, my grandfather apparently was insistent that everyone come home for Christmas. He was ill, of course, with some form of leukemia, although the reality of his condition wasn't discussed with the children, and he was gone the next month. He was 69 years old, which sounds so much younger to me now than it did at the time. I was 12, and was reminded that cancer kills loved ones, young and old.

I hadn't met Jennifer yet in the fall that my sister-in-law (we married twin brothers) was diagnosed with breast cancer, and my father and husband were both diagnosed with prostate cancer. There were a lot of surgeries going on that fall and spring. I also was preparing for my final doctoral defense, so a lot of that time is a blur. Over the next nine years, my sister-in-law went through the surgeries, the chemotherapy, the radiation, over and over, continuing to teach school, needing to take a break from teaching, returning to work, leaving work. She had a goal to see her son graduate from high school, and she even lived to see him complete his undergraduate years and meet his future partner. At her funeral, one of her close friends told a story about talking with her toward the end and saying she had hoped for a miracle. My sister-in-law told her the miracle was that she had the past nine years. I always thought of her as the glue that held my husband's side of the family together, although she had married into it. There are photos of her taken at Halloween one week before she died, shockingly jaundiced, but smiling so joy-fully with her daughter, son-in-law, son, and two tiny grandchildren. Somehow we all knew the day we needed to get down to her home in southern Illinois, or somehow she was able to hang on until we all arrived, because two hours after our family arrived and one hour after her best friends walked in, she was gone.

There are a number of my family members who have had vari-ous cancers that required surgeries and ongoing, annoying medical interventions, but for the most part, those lives go on in a fairly "normal" way. The obvious exceptions are those who have dealt with metastatic disease.

I've seen how this can end. Cancer can kill the young and old, men and women, the virtuous and unsavory, and it can destroy slowly or quickly. The treatments are grueling. Bodies wear out.

What's different with Jen's response to the disease and treat-ment is that she doesn't let us forget that. She has used her reality to help educate the rest of us. The generation before me—at least in my family—avoids talking openly about health issues. It's private, it's unseemly, and "some things you just don't talk about." So it can be a bit of a surprise when an uncle dies, a grandfather dies, a cousin dies. In my husband's family, health updates are confus-ing and often inaccurate. Lesser problems are catastrophized and serious problems are not communicated accurately or clearly. It is hard to know what is going on, and hard to prepare oneself or one's family members.

Despite my prior experience with cancer, Jen's initial diagnosis still was shocking. She was so young; we celebrated her marriage and Corbin's birth. She had her whole life ahead of her, and I believed she was also going to carry on the good work after some of the rest of us had retired, right? In certain situations at work, I still find myself thinking, "If Jennifer were still working here, she could knock this (task) out of the park."

I value the updates she's willing to share with the rest of us. I always feel like I'm learning—about cancer, but also about living—and that she's being incredibly unselfish by making it possible for us to not be caught off-guard. I imagine the anger, frustration, and helplessness I feel when the news is discouraging are feelings shared by many of her friends and followers. When the news is more positive, I am greatly relieved, but it is hard to get to a place of feeling joyful or truly celebratory. Her posts, both about her own journey as well as those of other metastatic breast cancer patients, along with my own life experiences, remind me how this can end. I don't dwell on it every day, which of course is my luxury since I'm not the patient—at this point in time, anyway—but denial only works some of the time. I think about her mother, in particular, and how much we moms worry about our children's health and safety, even when there is no immediate threat, and even when those children are grown.

Don't get me wrong. I still hope for a miracle—man-made or otherwise. Just as a diagnosis of Hodgkins is not the death sentence it once was, I keep hoping for the breakthrough that will eradicate this disease for Jen and for generations of women to follow. But since I've seen that sometimes the only miracle we get is the time we have together now, I'm embracing that, and I'm grateful that she is allowing it. At the same time, I'm afraid, knowing this is the only miracle we are to expect.

Jan is another close colleague from Parkland College:

Several months after Jen had both breasts removed, she was fitted for the Cadillac of prosthetic breasts. She said they cost more than a traditional boob job. Shortly after she was fitted for them, Jen, Linda (from the previous entry), and I met for dinner at our favorite hangout. When I arrived, Jen greeted me with a hug and sat back in her chair with her shoulders pulled back, sort of thrusting her new breasts toward me. I was oblivious because I'm not used to staring at women's chests. Finally, she pointed out to me that something was different, and once I saw what it was, I couldn't help but stare at her new "accessories," as she calls them. I'm sure if anyone had been watching us, they would have wondered why I was staring at the chest of the lovely woman sitting across the table. We had a good laugh and talked about the wonderful qualities of her new breasts: They make a farting noise when she hugs someone, they fit perfectly into her old bras, they have holes to drain water so they can be worn while swimming, and there's a freckle on one in the exact location of a freckle that formerly resided on her original breast.

That night when we were in the parking lot saying our good-byes, I asked Jen if I could see one of her new "girls." Jen's not shy, so she pulled one out of the neck of her shirt. I held it in my hand and marveled at its weight, texture, its holes, and the freckle. It didn't even cross my mind what someone walking across the parking lot would think if they saw me. Here I was holding and squeezing a woman's breast (albeit it wasn't "attached"), laughing, and joking about it. Finally after I realized what I was doing, I checked out the parking lot like a spy to make sure someone wasn't watching us.

This story is an example of what I love about Jen and being friends with her. She's still the same witty and funny woman she was before her diagnosis and can find the humor (sometimes morbid) in almost any situation. Cancer hasn't taken that from her, but I do fear the day when a scan shows progression that she'll view as the start of a downhill slide. My fear is that I'll lose the person Jen has been: A woman who faces this horrible disease head-on and uses her experiences to teach others what a breast cancer diagnosis really means. I fear that cancer will win, not only by taking her from us, but also by whittling away the characteristics that make Jen who she is. That would be a tragic loss to those of us who know her, as well as for those who don't know her but have benefitted from her sharing her experiences with them.

———————————

Brandie is a young breast cancer patient diagnosed at 31—Stage IIB Breast Cancer:

I met Jen via an online chat board in September of 2007. We were both diagnosed with breast cancer. Both of us were young moms, and both of us were drafted into a horrific war at the same time. We soldiered on through our treatments and exchanged stories of our journeys . . . losing our hair, getting chemo brain, experiencing radiation burns, and many other side effects of treatment. I felt we were pretty much the same person. We experienced the same horrible emotions and were living the same journey...until finally we began to see the "light at the end of the tunnel." The "light" was freeing and a peace of mind for me—I was surviving this dreaded cancer. I was leaving this horrific darkness. The sun was beginning to shine, and the clouds were lifting. But Jen's "light" was different . . . her "light" was a semi-truck headed her way. She wasn't leaving this dark tunnel. Jen was diagnosed with Stage IV cancer, and the semi-truck was headed straight for her.

I cried for weeks after hearing about Jen's diagnosis. I was devastated beyond words. I didn't know what to say to her, and I certainly didn't know how to feel. I scheduled *another* full body scan right away—worried that maybe I was also Stage IV now. After all, Jen and I had been diagnosed in 2007 with the same Stage II cancer. I thought maybe I was just going to follow in her footsteps. My scan ended up coming back clear, and it's been clear every year since then. For five years now, I've been cancer free, but I don't have the nerve to celebrate. I am not "free"; I live in fear that I will be "Jen" one day.

I sob uncontrollably at times, imagining her reality. She lives knowing she is going to leave her son motherless. Leaving my children is my biggest fear. My kids and I are so close, and I am their entire world. I know Jen is devastated with this realization, too, and it breaks my heart that she has to live her life knowing this. Her life is filled with medical appointments, scans, blood work, chemotherapy, and fear. I get angry knowing this is how she has to spend her life. I often wonder if this will be me one of these days; am I being "mentored" now without even knowing it?

For the past two years, Jen has come to California to fulfill some of her bucket list items. In 2011 we went to *The Ellen DeGeneres Show* and arranged for her to meet Ellen. I sobbed in the studio audience that day as Ellen hugged her tightly. I thought this was it; now that her bucket list was fulfilled, she was going back home to die. I cried so hard thinking I was watching her experience her last happy moment. Thank you, God; Jen made it to 2012! That year Jen and Corbin flew out for Mother's Day weekend, and we went to Disneyland with our boys. We had so much fun and laughed so hard, but at night, when I was lying in bed, I would cry, wondering if this was her last Mother's Day. Are these pictures I'm taking of her and her son, so happy and filled with love, her last? It was a heart-wrenching trip to see her with her son. It was the first time I was able to meet Corbin, and I saw my own son in him. Our boys are the same age, and they sure love their Moms. I was devastated after Jen left; was this the last hug I would give her? Was this the last time I would see her son happy and unscathed by trauma?

Knowing Jen has certainly given me a fear deeper than I even thought possible. I was devastated enough with my own diagnosis and having to live through chemotherapy, radiation, and a double mastectomy. At the time, going through all of that seemed to be my greatest nightmare. I believed I had already experienced fear to the deepest degree. But living through Jen's current journey brings the definition of fear to a whole new level. Her reality is my greatest fear. When she posts an update on Facebook, I tremble and cannot read it without crying. When she texts me, I can barely read her message. Is this going to be it? The fear is constant. I fear for Jen—and I fear for me. Not only do I fear I will end up with a Stage IV diagnosis, but I also fear having to handle Jen's passing. I simply cannot prepare myself for that day. Jen is my sister. We are one. I cannot bear to bury my friend, my comrade. I live in fear.

Ashley is my best friend—whom I met after my diagnosis:

I will never forget the first time Jen asked me to come over to her house to hang out. She invited me to a neighborhood cookout that she had organized. That date, October 25th, was always a hard day for me. It was the anniversary of my Nana's (my maternal grandmother) death from breast cancer. I recognized that I would be sensitive because of the date and because Jen had breast cancer, so I made up a ridiculous excuse and refused Jen's offer. I'd like to think that it wouldn't have mattered if Jen was healthy, that I would have refused an invitation from any friend that day, but I know I was very aware that day that Jen had breast cancer, the disease that had killed my Nana.

Luckily, Jen didn't give up on me and she invited me out again and we quickly became great friends. I learned there was so much more to Jen than what went through my mind on October 25th, 2009. Before I knew it, the fact that Jen had cancer was irrelevant to me. We often talked about our days, boys, work, weekend plans, working out, what to wear, etc. It also became normal to discuss chemotherapy treatments and scan results. I quickly realized that Jen was living a "normal" lifestyle and I would treat her as a "normal" friend. I knew what I was getting myself into; I was becoming best friends with someone with incurable cancer. But I didn't care that Jen had been given a terminal diagnosis. Her reality was that this cancer was not curable, and it would ultimately take her life. I knew that nobody lives forever and that we all have our own expiration dates. Instead of fearing for the day I would lose Jen or any of my loved ones, my relationship with Jen showed me how important it is to truly live every day.

I will never tell you that it is easy. Every time Jen goes in for a scan, I am scared to death. For that one day, while Jen is having the scan done, my mind is only on one thing—waiting, praying, hoping, believing—but not talking about it until I know the results. I can't bring myself to talk about it with anyone else; it is too terrifying to speak about the unknown. I don't want to have to deal with the "what ifs" unless I am smacked in the face with that reality. It is such a sense of relief when I get the call or text letting me know that there is little or no progression! Knowing that for the next three months, I can breathe easy before doing this all over again. I was talking to a new friend of mine after receiving the news of a new tumor in Jen's ribs, but overall stability. My new friend had met Jen only once, but hears me talk about her all the time. Her reaction to the news surprised me. I was celebrating and excited for minimal progression, and my friend looked at me baffled, and sad. It made me wonder, when did "not horrible news" become "great news"?

I wish there was reason to celebrate after every scan, but the reality is that sometimes we have to deal with the bad news. Every time there is progression, I have to figure out the best way to grieve for myself and for Jen, then turn around and be sure to be the rock that she needs. I'll admit, I am in complete denial; the only way that I am able to get through these moments and be strong for Jen is to deny myself the acceptance that the cancer in her body will actually take her life one day. I know the statistics; I know what other people go through. I know cancer is taking over her body, but I won't accept it is killing her. This is the only way to get through it for me. I don't accept that breast cancer will be terminal for my friend; I need her too much. Jen has always tried to protect the people around her; she shows strength whether she feels strong or not. I won't truly grieve for Jen, unless there is something to grieve about. In my heart, if I am grieving for Jen, I am giving up on her. I refuse to give up.

It is hard being Jen's friend, watching her go through so much, seeing her hurting and suffering, but being strong for those around her. I can't pretend to understand the thoughts and feelings that she has. I haven't been there; I haven't gone through this traumatic experience from her perspective. There are days, many days, that I have thoughts of how unfair this is. I try to understand why this would happen to such a wonderful person. I ask God why He would do this to Jen and her family. I don't have an answer, and I will never understand why, but I have strong faith, and I know that God has a plan and is changing the world with Jen. Jen has changed my life, I am not perfect, but I am a better person because of her. Jen has made me so much more aware of the blessings in my life. I have a better outlook on my life because I am friends with Jen. The importance of my life and of those around me has been magnified, and the challenges I face are put into better perspective.

I made a significant decision with my life because of my friendship with Jen. I picked up and moved across the country because I knew there is never a better time than now. The decision to move away from Jen and the neighborhood that we shared was extremely difficult. Jen was excited for me, but also sad that I would choose to leave her. I understood her perspective completely, and after a hard, emotional conversation we had about the fact Jen was dying and I was leaving, I emailed her the next day to say, "I feel incredibly guilty leaving you here, and it is obviously something I think about all the time. I wouldn't go if I didn't think you had an amazing support system here and know that it is the right thing for me to do. It is the craziest thing I have ever done, and I am trusting God that it is the right thing for me. I don't want it to feel like I am leaving you; I want it to show you how much you have taught me about living the short life we have been given." That is truly how I felt; it wasn't healthy for either of us to stay content in our lifestyles while we waited for Jen to die. I had to take advantage of my ability to take on a new adventure. I knew it wouldn't be the same living in a new city away from Jen, but I was willing to take that chance and make more of an effort to support Jen from over 800 miles away. I don't think I would have done it without Jen and her motivation to live her life to the fullest.

I am so lucky to have Jen in my life and to have shared so many memories of dream vacations, the pursuit of meeting Jen's idols, random road trips, and even lazy nights in watching movies and award shows. We are always talking and planning our next excursion and continue to make new memories all the time no matter where we live. The hardest part is thinking about the future events in my life that I will need her to be there for. I often wonder if Jen will be standing next to me at my wedding, or if she will at least know and give the BFF stamp of approval for this future man. Who will I call to gossip with and tell my secrets to? Will Jen be here to meet my children? My mind honestly just will not accept the thought of Jen's not being there. I can't process the emotions of her not being there for every major milestone in my future; it is too much for me to fathom. My heart hurts when I think, even for a short time what the reality could be. There is no way I can prepare for the day that Jen isn't a quick phone call away. I won't give up on her; Jen is in my life forever.

"I desperately wanted to enjoy this incredible time with my *family* and not let my mind go to that **dark place**, imagining the vacations they will go on without me."

FREAKING OUT

EVER since I was diagnosed with cancer, I often get asked, "How are you doing?" But there is no easy answer to this question. There isn't a simple, concise answer that I can usually offer, so my standard reply has become, "I'm okay." But the truth is sometimes, I am not okay. Sometimes, in fact, I am beginning my descent into freaking out or am already deep in the pits of its black abyss. If I were to answer authentically and honestly, I'd reply, "I'm simply trying to *stay alive*." People could reply, "Well, aren't we all?"

The times when I'm freaking out, I'm overcome with a crushing panic and dark, anxiety-filled thoughts. I become haunted by the fear of my own future. When I'm freaking out, it isn't over a missed bill or speeding ticket. It is literally about life and death, specifically *my* life and death. People often say, "Well, you look so good!" and while I know they mean well, I want to say, "I don't leave the house on bad days. I don't post those pictures on social media. I'm physically and emotionally exhausted from the end

41

of this cycle of chemotherapy. The exhaustion is the result of chemotherapy being cumulative, and I've been on it for over five years. I question if my body will give out from sheer exhaustion or if cancer will devour it. At this point, either one seems a possibility." Quite simply, it's a mind fuck. But, I try to control what the outside world witnesses, keeping the bad days hidden inside my safe place, my home. However, this is written in my safe space during one of those bad days.

I should first explain that treatment for metastatic breast cancer is overwhelmingly difficult and grueling. It is considered "palliative" treatment because metastatic breast cancer is incurable, so the goal is to extend my life living with cancer. There are times that I think I just can't do it anymore. I am beyond exhausted with fatigue. Beyond weak. Beyond weary. My body is beaten down by thirteen straight days of oral chemotherapy and weekly chemotherapy infusions of an additional two drugs. Since the chemotherapy treatment wipes out my immune system, I have to self-inject daily shots of a white blood cell booster serum for three days following treatment. At this point, on a good day, I feel hung over. On a bad day, my thinking is muddled, my body has various aches and pains, and my stomach is sour most of the day. I sleep ten hours at night, get up, drop my son off at school, then often return home to sleep for another two hours. The fatigue is severe, so I never feel "rested." No amount of sleep seems to restore my energy. My stomach keeps cramping and is upset from all the oral chemotherapy I've had over the last two weeks. My appetite is almost non-existent, which isn't good because I really can't afford to lose weight.

Then there's freaking out about losing another friend to this disease. Last week, in fact, one of my local Stage IV friends just got out of the hospital. She was in for almost a week. She was hospitalized because of an infection, and her immune system was completely wiped out from the chemotherapy treatment. Her white blood cell count was zero when it should be over 4,500. She was diagnosed Stage IV two years after I was, and while I appreciate her friendship, it's also a hard one. I've watched too many friends die, and the slippery slope to their death usually starts with needing to be hospitalized for one issue or another. This friendship is also a unique one because I was diagnosed Stage IV first, so logically I should die first. But cancer isn't logical, and I imagine she's jealous that my body is failing more slowly than hers. Meanwhile, I'm terrified watching another friend die of the same damn disease that is annihilating my own body.

There's also the classic "scanxiety" freak-out. This is a unique kind of freak-out in which a person worries about what an upcoming scan or medical test will reveal—fearing the worst kind of news. Recently I went on a vacation with my entire family to the Beaches Resort in Turks and Caicos; it was a Christmas present from my parents. In an attempt to stay in the moment, I decided to go "unplugged." No phone. No email. No Facebook. I figured that the world would go on just fine without my being connected. A trip of this magnitude is not something our family regularly does. The last time we took a trip like this was in 2005, just after my maternal grandmother died. Her request to our family was to use some of the inheritance to take the family on a vacation, so we went to an all-inclusive resort in Jamaica. This time, we chose a family-friendly resort as Corbin and my nephew, Jaxson, would be with us. In the back of my mind I wondered if this vacation was planned in anticipation of my declining health and wanting to have one last great family moment before cancer gruesomely stole my body.

I desperately wanted to enjoy this incredible time with my family and not let my mind go to that dark place, where I imagined the vacations they would go on without me. I felt a responsibility to make it the best vacation possible, in case it was the last. Looking back, I want my family to remember those precious memories full of laughter and love. So I needed to work on grounding myself and truly being in the moment.

So there I was—on my unplugged family vacation—and amazingly being unplugged disconnected me from freaking out . . . until I got home and back to reality. I didn't want to get bad news and have to switch to a treatment that would be an even greater threat to my quality of life. I knew the number of chemotherapy options remaining were dwindling, and each one had significant side effects that would impair my quality of life. For a moment,

I felt relieved as I remembered that my oncologist and his staff always worked to quickly share the test results with me, but then I quickly began to freak out again. I thought about the cough I had while on vacation and wondered if the cancer had spread to my lungs. I worried about the pain in my back—trying to decide if it was from playing with Corbin or if the cancer was destroying more vertebrae. I started to overanalyze everything I felt in my body.

Adding to the dark thoughts entering my mind was the knowledge that I had a Positron Emission Tomography (PET) scan, upon returning from vacation. This scan would tell us if the five chemotherapies I had been taking were working. And it wasn't that I was scared of the test itself; after all, I've had over a dozen of these scans in the past five years, so I knew what to expect. I knew I would have to arrive at the cancer center on an empty stomach and then be injected with a radioactive tracer that identifies areas metabolizing sugar at a higher rate, such as cancer cells. I also knew that I would be contained in a room constructed from lead walls for an hour, allowing the radioactive tracer to stream through my body; then I would be instructed to empty my bladder and enter the room with the large machine that would scan me. Next, I would lie on the table, staying as still as possible while my body was moved in and out of a three-foot wide plastic hole. During the twenty-minute scan, three-dimensional images of my body would be formed for the radiologist to review. Finally, I knew that the areas with cancer, or "hot-spots," would glow and the radiologist would review the scan as well as measure the size, depth, and number of tumors present in my body.

And if the scan were to show that the current treatment of five chemotherapies wasn't working and that I had progression and more cancer throughout my body, I'd have to quickly switch to a new treatment in hopes of slowing the disease. The few remaining choices, however, all had a side-effect of severe neuropathy, which causes the nerves in my extremities, my hands and feet, to become numb. I've dealt with this side effect on previous chemotherapies, and the last time it was so severe that I couldn't open a water bottle because my hands were numb. Grasping a knife to cut an apple was difficult and dangerous. Typing was a slow and arduous process because I couldn't feel the keys on the keyboard. When visiting a friend and going for a boat ride, then floating in the lake, I had a difficult time climbing back into the boat because of my neuropathy. I struggled to grasp the ladder, pull myself up, and climb up with my feet. I was worried they would have to help pull me into the boat to get me back on board. I had trouble walking up stairs, and I could only wear flip-flops because anything else felt like I was walking with my feet buried in cement blocks. I started freaking out thinking this quality of life could soon be my reality again.

Such "scanxiety" is common in Stage IV cancer patients. It is heightened by knowing that bad news could be coming my way and that the remaining options would greatly impact my quality of life. Unfortunately I couldn't anticipate what the results would be . . . this summer was when I felt the "healthiest" I had in five-years, yet that's when the biggest progression, to my liver and one lung, was found.

The three-hour wait between the scan and getting the results is always emotionally brutal. My mind drifts and goes to a place of fear, the dark kind. I keep a supply of Ativan, an anti-anxiety drug, on standby in case the fears become near-paralyzing. I hyper-analyze everything I feel physically, but I've learned that I can't trust how I feel as a predictor of what the scan reveals. Feeling good (relatively speaking) doesn't mean that treatment is working at slowing the spread of cancer, so my mind wanders to those dark places where I imagine cancer spreading, annihilating bones and spreading to more vital organs in my body.

I have no choice but to wait hours for the results and learn what my future holds. As I wait, I see a reminder for my six-month appointment for the dentist. Six months from now seems like an eternity. It's a future date and time that I can't comprehend. I don't know if I'll be alive to have them check my teeth, or if it will be one of the many phone calls my family will have to make canceling appointments due to my death.

If the scan shows things are stable, I will stay on this same treatment of five chemotherapies. If there is progression, then a long and serious conversation about quality of life and treatment will occur with my oncologist. I literally trust this man with my life; I just wish science was creating more options he could offer.

Regardless of the results, there will be another scan in another three months, and I will be freaking out, all over again.

"While I struggled with *leaving* this piece of my identity behind, I realized that I am still *educating*, outside the classroom, to the many lives of those living with metastatic breast cancer."

EDUCATING

WHEN I was a child, I always dreamed of being a teacher when I grew up. I was excited when teachers would discard their old textbooks so that I could take them to "teach" my younger siblings. I even had a chalkboard to ensure that my version of school, which took place in my bedroom, closely matched my school environment. I loved standing by the chalkboard and educating my siblings, friends, or even stuffed animals.

When I applied to college, though, I didn't go in to the education field; instead I decided to combine my love of helping others with my love of sports. I discovered my joy in helping others in high school when I went on a go-and-serve trip with my church youth group while volunteering for the Appalachia Service Project. In the remote hills of the Appalachian Mountains, I worked to make homes warmer, safer, and drier for those living in severe poverty. I also discovered my love of sports in high school. Although I wasn't athletically gifted, I enjoyed being on a team and helping. I was then accepted into the athletic training program at Southern Illinois University and began the rigorous schedule of classes and hours of rehabbing injuries, taping ankles, and stretching players in the training room. In just two years, I had over 1,100 hours of working with the athletes in the training room, at practice, and at games.

After those two years and one horrific car accident that took the life of my college roommate's younger brother, I knew that my career needed to be more about helping people and less about rehabbing injuries. Still, I didn't pursue a career in education. I switched my major to social work, taking up to 21 credit hours per semester to graduate on time. I excelled in class, earning straight As throughout my junior and senior years. After graduating, I immediately started working on my Master of Social Work degree from The Jane Addams College of Social Work at the University of Illinois at Chicago.

I was accepted into the accelerated program, which meant a normal two-year program was condensed into one year. The program required being a full-time student and an unpaid intern. My concentration was in Child and Family Therapy. I carefully selected my internship agency, aiming to work with at-risk youth. During my internship, I worked in private counseling with a number of youth on probation. I also worked with a group of students at an alternative high school. All had been expelled from their former high schools due to behavioral issues and truancy. One of our first group sessions was, essentially, "educate the white girl from central Illinois about your life as an inner city youth." I learned about gangs, drug wars, unemployment, distrust of the police, and lack of family support. In that one session, they taught me more than any textbook I'd read.

One student I worked with was Kevin. He was a scrawny, white, 14 year-old male. He talked about the confidence and sense of power he felt when flashing a gun to rival gang members. He talked about his drug-addicted mother, incarcerated brother, and complete lack of knowledge regarding his father. I vividly remember asking Kevin, "Where do you see yourself in five years?" He matter-of-factly replied, "Locked up, or six feet under." Kevin saw himself with no future.

At the time he said this, I was 22 and couldn't fathom how an adolescent could envision such a hopeless future. Only now, after my Stage IV diagnosis, can I understand and relate to Kevin's inability to see a future. My life is lived in three-month segments, from one scan to the next. Every three months, the scans show if the current treatment is working, or if the cancer has outsmarted yet another drug therapy and modern medicine has failed me again. I have lived this way for over four years, so I've lost the ability to see the big events yet to come. Cancer stole that from me, but I also realized it's out of self-preservation. If I attempted to daydream of the future, the nightmare of my reality would quickly return, reminding me that those daydreams are just that ... dreams.

Growing up, I never dreamed that I would return to my hometown. I enjoyed my work with the youth in Chicago, but when I graduated, I wanted to be closer to my family, so I returned to my roots. I found security and comfort in a familiar setting.

One Sunday, I saw an employment ad in the local newspaper for a Student Development Advocate at Parkland College. I was somewhat familiar with Parkland College because I took a few summer classes there to make up for switching majors halfway through college. I refreshed my resume and submitted my application. After I was scheduled for an interview, I researched potential questions to ask, and carefully thought through my possible answers to their questions.

The interview was in a small room in front of a committee, including a department chair, two full-time faculty members, my potential office mate, and my potential boss. It was completely intimidating as a twenty-four year-old recent graduate. I learned the position would be working with at-risk students. This was a new position and a new concept in the community college world. It was a blend of academic advising and case management. Parkland College has an open-door admission policy, so all students who have graduated from high school, or earned a G.E.D., were accepted. However, that doesn't mean that all students are ready for college-level classes. This position, the Student Development Advocate, would work with the students who assessed in the lower-level reading class, typically reading at a 7th–9th grade level. Even though I had the academic qualifications, I didn't have a lot of work experience since I was only a year out of graduate school.

In recalling the initial interview, the committee chair, and now Vice President for Student Services at Parkland, Dr. Linda Hamman Moore, wrote:

"We interviewed at least three finalists. Seriously, all of them were qualified and had relevant experience. The other candidates did not bomb their interviews, but there was something about Jennifer's energy, genuineness, and promise. Obviously, she did not have as much relevant experience as the other candidates, given her youth, but the education and experience she had were meaningful. These committee members knew our students and the population she would be working with, and she seemed completely open to learning and supervision.

I heard a speaker at a conference, who categorized employees as mercenaries or heroes. (He cited Joseph Campbell.) The mercenaries might do good work, but there's always going to be that "What are you going to give me for it?" element. The heroes hear the call and take on the challenge, even when they might not want to go through all of the trials. I think the committee instinctively knew Jennifer was cut from the hero cloth, and they knew the only type of employee who could rise to the challenges of being a Student Development Advocate and working with our most academically at-risk students had to be an eternally optimistic hero. I think that's what the committee responded to in selecting Jennifer."

About a week after the interview, I was offered, and gladly accepted, the position. My career at Parkland began. I learned my way around the 750,000 square foot college, which most say is built like a maze. I met the new colleagues I would work with while I focused on the population I would serve. I was trained in academic advising for this student population. And then I was given enough rope to hang myself . . . but I didn't! I connected with these students, learning about them as individuals, hearing their dreams and desires.

It wasn't always easy, and at times I questioned if I was truly making a difference in the lives of these students. Many of the students I worked with were youth from inner-city Chicago. Their families saw Parkland College, located in a university town, as a safe haven to get their kids off the streets. One day I learned a former student was murdered in Chicago over a pair of sneakers. I was asked to write a eulogy on behalf of his time at Parkland College. I watched the destruction of many youth as the evils of their past crept into their present. Reality taught me that my role in their lives was often minor. I was being educated on how, as a society, we are creatures of habit and often return to what is comfortable and known, just as I returned to my hometown after graduation.

One group of students I worked closely with was the basket-ball team, and many of the players were from inner-city Chicago, and had a mentality similar to Kevin. They saw basketball, or the streets, as their future. Education was essentially a consequence of playing at the next level. After earning the respect of the team, one player said, "Hey, can you bring your boyfriend? I want to see what it takes to date a girl like you." After a game a few weeks later, the same player said, "Wow, I didn't know your boyfriend was so old!" I laughed as I explained to him it was my dad with me at the game, not my boyfriend. Although I was only a few years older than the majority of the students I worked with, I had created solid boundaries and the students respected my role at the college. I unknowingly educated them about how to treat a woman.

The Student Development Advocate position was funded by a grant, and when the state abruptly stopped funding the position, the Vice President, at the time, literally pulled out a calculator. He reviewed how many students I had contact with, how many credit hours they attempted, and their persistence rate. He simply said, "Well, the job pays for itself," and luckily I was absorbed into the permanent payroll.

Since the concept of student development advocacy was new in community colleges, we presented this approach at several conferences. At the National Association for Developmental Education (NADE) conference in St. Louis, we had a standing-room-only crowd of fellow professionals from across the country. We explained the theory and rationale behind creating the position. We discussed the number of student contacts I had and the incomparable dedication this position required. We also knew that, if we had funding, we could expand services and help more students. So Parkland

College applied for, and was awarded, a 5-year, $1.6 million dollar U.S. Department of Education Title III grant. I applied for, and was named the director of the grant, overseeing two Student Development Advocates (my former role), a technology specialist, and an educational specialist. All members of the team were dedicated to educating the at-risk student population in various ways to help them become successful students.

While there were often struggles and heartbreak watching students revert to their former lifestyles rather than make school their first priority, there were often moments of pure bliss. I saw many students achieve their dream of earning a degree. I beamed like a proud family member when, against all odds, they walked across the stage at graduation. I was a witness to their determination and ultimate success.

I worked with hundreds of students each semester, including the student athletes. In working with the athletic staff, we realized there was a large need for the student athletes to get acclimated to campus, as well as learn what resources were available, how to best manage their time as a student and an athlete, and how to maintain their eligibility. We created an athlete-only section of an education, career, and life planning class. I led the development of the class and taught a section each fall, in addition to my regular duties. My childhood dream of being a teacher had come true, even if it was teaching just one class a semester.

I searched for different ways to educate the students, especially about goal setting. One of the assignments was called, "Remember Me, Now and Then." The students had to each write two personal eulogies, one as if they died at that very moment in time and one at their future date of death. Many of the students revolted against this assignment saying it was disturbing to think about their death. The idea of death and dying seems to be one society, in general, struggles with. The purpose of the assignment was for them to reflect on what achievements they had already accomplished and set goals for what they hoped to complete. I didn't ask the students to do something I wasn't comfortable with; I wrote my own eulogies and presented them to the class. However, like many of the students in the class, I didn't feel an emotional attachment to what I wrote; I was still under the illusion of immortality. Little did I know that just two years later I would be diagnosed and think about death and dying on a consistent basis.

When I was initially diagnosed in 2007, the students in my class all wore pink on the day of my surgery. I was a dedicated employee and continued to work while going through treatment, often bringing my laptop and working remotely from the chemotherapy room. When the cancer returned and continued to spread, my body felt as if it could collapse from sheer exhaustion. I looked at my responsibilities, first, being a mom to Corbin. Second, being a full-time metastatic cancer patient in treatment for the rest of my life, however brief or lengthy it may be. The responsibilities of a professional cancer patient included staying educated by researching the latest treatment options, maintaining various doctor appointments, attending ongoing chemotherapy sessions, and trying to allow my body to rest. I had to continue on in treatment in hopes of extending my life. Although it was a blow to my ego, I realized that Parkland College would continue on just fine without me. I was replaceable in my job there. I am *not* replaceable as Corbin's mom.

So, statistically when I should have been dead, I left my dream job at Parkland College in hopes of extending my life. This decision was a heartbreaking one to make. I had to give up my career, which I loved, to try and stay alive. I mourned the loss of this giant piece of my identity. While many who are diagnosed with early stage breast cancer continue to work, or resume work after treatment, I knew this was a final good-bye to my career. I knew I'd miss the intellectual stimulation I had working with forward-thinking individuals. I also knew that leaving my career and going on disability would impact my financial situation greatly as I would only earn half of my salary. I would also have to go on COBRA health insurance. While the premium for COBRA is expensive, it is a small price to pay for the treatments I require to extend my life.

When I left Parkland, I maintained several close professional relationships with the staff. I had worked at Parkland for nearly a decade, and making the choice to leave was an extremely difficult one. My job was a huge piece of who I was and fulfilled my desire to educate others. When I left, I struggled losing this piece of my identity and wondered if I would be forgotten. I still attended athletic events and went to the grand opening of the new gym. The desperately-needed makeover was stunning. The gym was now brightly lit, showing off the new green and gold paint. There was a new hardwood floor with the cobra mascot emblem painted on the center of it. There were new bleachers offering comfortable backrests, compared to the old wooden bleachers where you'd risk getting a splinter. There was excitement in the air at the unveiling. While at the grand opening, the athletic director pulled me aside and said, "I can now officially tell you, you've been nominated and selected for the Parkland College Athletic Hall of Fame for 2011." I was in absolute shock. Each year, in addition to inducting former star athletes, they also induct a "contributor" who played a significant part in working with the athletic department and their student athletes.

On February 11, 2012, Parkland College welcomed back the 2005 NJCAA World Series Runners-Up baseball team, as well as a former coach, and four other athletes who went on to have successful careers at four-year institutions. My tall, lanky, uncoordinated body was surrounded by former athletes, and at half time we had to walk to the center of the court, one-by-one, to accept our awards.

As I walked, the announcer read:

"Jennifer has been one of the Cobra's most ardent supporters on and off the field, regularly attending Parkland games and

fundraising events. Jennifer helped develop the athlete sections of Psychology 109 "Strategies for Success" and assisted with incoming athlete orientation, academic advising, and coordination of on-campus recruiting visits. She also had the vision for the "It's a Parkland Thing" ad campaign, featuring PC athletes from area high schools. Jennifer and her son, Corbin, live in Champaign."

Thankfully, walking to midcourt, I had the most handsome escort possible. Corbin decided he wanted to walk with me, holding hands. By chance he ended up on my left side, so I was looking at him and missed a standing ovation from my former colleagues as we walked across the floor. Those standing were the ones who educated me in my near decade long career at Parkland College. By the grace of God, neither of us tripped. I accepted the award, smiled for a picture, then was able to face the crowd—a sea of so many former coworkers and students with smiles on their faces and tears in their eyes. It was a powerful visual testament to the work I had done during my career at Parkland.

So, while my career wasn't as a traditional teacher in a classroom, it truly was in educating as I worked with thousands of students during my career at Parkland. While working with at-risk students wasn't always easy, being an employee for a supportive, forward-thinking, inclusive, educating college was an incredible opportunity.

While I struggled with leaving this piece of my identity behind, I realized that I am still educating, but outside the classroom. I am educating and bringing true awareness about the realities of metastatic breast cancer. I am still driven to educate others, but now the subject is metastatic breast cancer and the content is how to truly *live* with a terminal diagnosis.

Part of my job as a professional cancer patient is to educate others. But, I also spend time exposing companies that are exploiting breast cancer, and the pink ribbon, purely for their own profit. A lot of them appear to "celebrate" Breast Cancer Awareness Month, but send little or no money to a cancer organization. But what's to celebrate about a life-threatening disease, whose treatments amount to slash, burn, and poison? Note, I said disease and not "sickness," because that would imply that I'm contagious or that I will get better. As much as I believe in miracles, I also know the cruel reality of this disease. Cancer is a thief and murderer, not a "sickness."

I seize the chance to speak at national conferences, or be the guest lecturer for 200+ students in a community health class at the University of Illinois. I educate the students on the truths of breast cancer and help them learn how important it is that they know their own bodies.

I passionately participated in educating others about metastatic breast cancer when I submitted my presentation for the Pecha Kucha chat in Champaign. The format allows each presenters to have 20 slides, 20 seconds per slide, with the slides automatically advancing. In front of 400+ people, and in less than seven minutes, I educated the audience about living with metastatic breast cancer.

I have also helped create, plan, and implement the *You Are Not Alone Symposium* for young women with breast cancer. The day-long program featured sessions on genetics, nutrition, talking to your children about your diagnosis, prostheses, yoga, living with metastatic disease, and more.

I also make sure that I am educating others who are newly diagnosed with metastatic breast cancer. I find connections through the community, Imerman Angels, and social media. Educating, whether it's hundreds of students in a lecture, or a young mom newly diagnosed with breast cancer, will remain my absolute passion.

"Pinkwasher: (pink'-wah-sher) noun: A company or organization that claims to care about breast cancer by promoting a *pink ribbon* product, but at the same time produces, manufactures and/or sells products that are linked to the *disease*."

PINK-WASHING

FOR those of us in *cancerland*, October is known as "Pinktober." In the beginning, the intention of Pinktober was good: It
was about raising awareness and funds to eradicate breast cancer. Then, however, capitalism snuck into the pink picture. Now,
countless companies add pink ribbons to their products for breast
cancer awareness month in order to make bigger profits; and this
phenomenon is called Pink-Washing®. Breast Cancer Action coined
the term Pinkwasher® in 1992 as part of their Think Before You
Pink® campaign. Pinkwasher: (pink'-wah-sher) noun: A company or
organization that claims to care about breast cancer by promoting a
pink ribbon product, but at the same time produces, manufactures
and/or sells products that are linked to the disease. BCAction states
that any contribution, no matter the amount, making money off
the backs of women who are dying from this disease is wrong, and
the noise companies make to sell these products distracts from the
real work needed to address and end a disease that has reached an

epidemic scale in this country. The bigger concern, according to BCAction, is regarding the products that contain ingredients that may contribute to this disease; hence, the hypocrisy.

Many companies even manufacture or sell products that contain known carcinogens. Let me get this straight: A company wants to support people with breast cancer by giving them breast cancer? Take, for example, the pharmaceutical giant Eli Lilly, one of the most egregious pinkwashers to date. Breast Cancer Action launched the campaign "Milking Cancer" to expose Eli Lilly, the world-wide manufacturer and distributor of a synthetic cancer-linked chemical called recombinant bovine growth hormone (rBGH or rBST). This chemical is given to cows to stimulate milk production. It's been linked to breast cancer and other health problems. In fact, it has been banned entirely in Canada, Australia, Japan, and all countries in the European Union. In 2008, Eli Lilly acquired rBGH, sold as Posilac, from the biotech company Monsanto—despite the bad reputation Monsanto has acquired over the years for their flagrant disregard for public health and insidious business practices. Eli Lilly acquired rBGH from Monsanto, knowing that Monsanto's own studies show that milk from cows treated with rBGH/Posilac contains increased levels of IGF-1, a hormone linked to an increased risk of cancer. So check this out:

1. Eli Lilly creates and sells a cancer linked product.

2. Eli Lilly sells a cancer treatment chemotherapy drug called Gemzar, and a drug, Evista, to reduce the risk of breast cancer in women who are at high risk of being diagnosed with the disease; drugs which brought in $2,683,000,000 for the company in 2008.

Bottom line? As BCAction boldly states: Eli Lilly is milking cancer.

But so are countless cosmetic and personal care companies who use parabens in their products. Parabens (ethylparaben, butylparaben, methylparaben, and propylparaben) are chemical preservatives used to fight bacteria and fungus in products such as shampoo, body lotion, toothpaste, and shaving gel. They are included in beauty and personal care products to extend the shelf life of products; however, parabens are also estrogen-mimickers and bind to estrogen receptors on cells. They are absorbed through the skin, blood, and digestive system and have been found in breast cancer tissue. A 2011 study by Science Daily, "Parabens in Breast Tissue Not Limited to Women Who Have Used Underarm Products," showed at least one paraben was present in 99% of breast cancer biopsies and 60% of the samples had all five parabens. Since then, consumer awareness has increased and some companies have reformulated their products without parabens. In fact, cosmetic giant Aveda went paraben-free due to consumer demand. Want to know what is in your personal care products? Check out the Skin Deep Cosmetics Database at http://safecosmetics.org.

But, pinkwashing isn't limited to pharmaceutical and personal care companies. The athletic sportswear company Lucy Activewear came out with "breast cancer awareness" clothing in fall 2012. This line of clothing included five pink athletic tops ranging from tank tops to long sleeve tops and pink running shorts, which cost anywhere from $29-$65. When a breast cancer activist asked Lucy Activewear what percentage of sales from the line would be donated and which charity they would go to, the company responded, *"I regret to inform you that we don't have an affiliation with any charities at this time including BCA [Breast Cancer Awareness]; however, we do hope to in the future."* Breast cancer awareness started more than thirty years ago, yet this company creates active wear with a pink ribbon and *hopes* to have an affiliation with a charity in the future? You've got to be kidding me.

Research has shown that a majority of consumers would purchase an item associated with a good cause, such as breast cancer awareness. The buyer has the impression they have helped the cause by buying the particular product, but I can tell you that my friends are still dying, and it isn't for lack of awareness. We are aware; we are saturated in pink products during Pinktober. Now, we *MUST* move beyond awareness to action.

What's interesting is that the original breast cancer awareness ribbon wasn't even pink: It was a pale peach color. BCAction's website chronicles the history of the pink ribbon. The original concept was created in 1992, in fact, by 68 year-old Charlotte

Haley. While Haley had not been diagnosed with breast cancer, her mother, grandmother, and daughter were all diagnosed with the disease. She made peach-colored ribbons in her home and attached them to index cards that stated, "The National Cancer Institute annual budget is $1.8 billion, and only 5 percent goes for cancer prevention. Help us wake up our legislators and America by wearing this ribbon." Then *Self* magazine contacted Haley and offered to partner with her effort to bring more awareness to breast cancer. Maybe Haley predicted the future and saw our capitalist society completely commercializing the pink ribbon under the guise of "awareness." Haley declined the offer, saying they were too commercial. So the magazine then teamed up with cosmetic giant Estee Lauder. The cosmetic corporation turned to their attorneys for advice. The attorneys stated they simply needed to change the color of the ribbon. After a few focus groups, they decided pink was the perfect color for the breast cancer awareness ribbon. The color pink was soft, feminine, and evoked a sense of hope. What part, though, of breast cancer is soft or feminine? If I would have been included in a focus group, I would have told them I see none of those things when I see a pink ribbon; instead, I see a noose as this disease strangles my hope for a future.

There are some remarkable cancer-related charities (see Jen's Top Ten in the back for my favorites); however some repulsive and shocking pink items have been created for profit.

What does Pinktober do to raise awareness of people living with Stage IV disease? What about the people who will never be cured? Who will never be called survivors? The pink ribbons most often celebrate the people who've made it to the other side of breast cancer. We should celebrate these women for their smarts, their courage, their determination, their anger. But we will not celebrate a disease that kills them. We must not forget those who are being left behind—the people who are still dying from this disease. These women, like me, who are dying from this disease didn't "fail" by not trying hard enough or not staying positive. Modern medicine failed these women because there still is not a cure for breast cancer.

Mahatma Gandhi said, "A nation's greatness is measured by how it treats its weakest members." So how is Pinktober treating peoples with metastatic disease? Are we being overlooked? Aren't we in most need? What's more: Out of all of the money that is raised for breast cancer research, only 2% goes to metastatic breast cancer research, yet 30% of people diagnosed with breast cancer progress to a Stage IV diagnosis. The weakest members are given the fewest resources and fewest reasons to truly hope.

Since the late 1980s, more than 40,000 women and a couple thousand men die each year from breast cancer. It is as if the death toll from September 11th keeps happening each month, year after year. In this case, the terrorists aren't on planes; they are rogue cells that rapidly duplicate and grow resistant to treatments. A tragedy the size of September 11th was not turned in to simple awareness;

it turned in to a call to action on terrorism. The way our culture approaches breast cancer should be the same, and we must critically question Pinktober as a way to raise to awareness and eradicate the disease. Awareness won't stop people from getting this disease. We need better treatment options for women, like me, who are living with metastatic breast cancer. We need strong environmental reform to stop people from being diagnosed in the first place. We need to take serious steps to address the root causes of health inequities that move beyond screening and healthcare access.

In order to truly move forward, we need to support women living with breast cancer, while also working towards prevention for future generations. Searching for a cure has led to the stalemate that mainstream breast cancer organizations have had for more than 30-years. We need to expose companies that are purely capitalizing on the epidemic of breast cancer. We also need to become aware of pinkwashing. Most of all, we need to stop exploiting people with the disease, and as BCAction states, *think before you pink*.

"We created memories as we painted the town red, or pink, because of *friendship*, not because of *cancer*."

CONNECTING

I consider myself a Professional Cancer Patient (PCP). One of my responsibilities as a PCP is to know what is happening in the field of breast cancer. This means learning about what clinical trials are available, what new treatments are being approved by the FDA, and what research is being conducted for possible breakthroughs. In addition to knowing what scientists, researchers, and doctors are doing, I try to be aware of how other breast cancer patients—both private and public figures—are navigating their own diagnoses.

Young women diagnosed with breast cancer are of particular importance to me because I was diagnosed at such a young age (30), and while indulging in one of my delicious, but guilty pleasures, I learned that Giuliana Rancic, a host for E! News, was diagnosed with breast cancer at age 36. I started to research her biography. I learned that Giuliana, like me, struggled with something I was all too familiar with: Infertility. There is a two-tier approach with infertility patients. The common first treatment is Intra Uterine

Insemination (IUI), which in laypersons terms is the "turkey baster" approach. The more intensive procedure is In-Vitro Fertilization (IVF), which translates to combining the sperm and egg in a petri dish, and then several days later, implanting the embryo(s) back into the woman—a "test tube baby." In Giuliana's attempt to go through a third cycle of IVF, her doctor ordered a full physical, including a mammogram. That mammogram revealed a suspicious area, which led to the biopsy and diagnosis of breast cancer. While Giuliana originally had a lumpectomy, the surgery didn't remove all of the cancer, so she decided to have a bilateral mastectomy with immediate reconstruction. She was diagnosed at an early stage, meaning the cancer hadn't spread, and her doctor did not recommend chemotherapy; just Tamoxifen, an anti-estrogen pill, for five years.

The issue of infertility, manipulating and increasing a woman's hormones, and breast cancer, which is often fueled off those very hormones, has been actively debated. Infertility treatment is still relatively new; the first successful birth of a test tube baby was in 1978 in the UK. In the 35 years since that birth, there has been much debate regarding religious and ethical standards of infertility treatment. Research extends back over a couple of decades; however, there is not a definitive correlation, yet. For every study that shows an increased risk of breast cancer after infertility treatment, there is another study showing no increased risk.

Giuliana and I are not alone in the infertility diagnosis then breast cancer diagnosis. I've met more than a dozen other young women who were treated for infertility, then diagnosed with breast cancer at a young age. Each story makes me believe there is a stronger connection than research has shown. With infertility treatment being relatively new to mainstream society, and accessible for those with health insurance that covers it, I don't think we have an accurate grasp on how manipulating hormones impacts a woman's health in the long term.

And while the diagnosis of breast cancer is horrific, the diagnosis of and treatment for infertility can be just as grueling: emotionally as well as physically. There is no month dedicated to "infertility awareness." There aren't walks and runs raising money for infertility research. There is no ribbon to raise awareness and hope for people struggling with infertility. It is such a private, lonely, intimate struggle.

Knowing that Giuliana had been through a similar experience with infertility, a miscarriage, and breast cancer diagnosis, I felt I knew Giuliana in a way the general public did not. Our lifestyles are so different, her living in Los Angeles, dressing in designer clothes; me living in central Illinois, most often found in jeans and a t-shirt. Although our daily lives are incredibly different, I had experienced the same thoughts, fears, and emotions since I also experienced infertility, a miscarriage, and a breast cancer diagnosis. These thoughts and fears are what made me feel connected to her. I tuned in to her reality show with her husband called, *Giuliana and Bill*, on the Style Network, and watched as cameras documented their life. The cameras captured her emotional journey with infertility in earlier seasons. I tuned in as she went through the appointments, surgery, and decision-making process for her breast cancer diagnosis. Although Giuliana's story aired on TV, I felt connected to her because I remembered the emotions that go along with making decisions regarding a breast cancer diagnosis at a young age. I could relate to her sense of fear and uncertainty, as well as her determination to move forward in life and be a mother. I also learned that they were hosting a Season Finale viewing party at their restaurant, RPM Italian, in Chicago.

After learning about the party, I emailed three well-connected friends from college and wrote, "I know it's an unlikely possibility, but is there any chance one of you has a connection to the Season Finale party of *Giuliana and Bill* at RPM Italian on June 8th?" Thankfully, one of my three friends, Erica Strama, named one of *Today's Chicago Women* "It Girls," knew the right person to contact. I don't play the "cancer card" often, but when I do, I go for grand moments, and I sensed this would be one of them. And, I was right; the cancer card got me a ticket to attend the Season Finale party of *Giuliana and Bill* at their restaurant in Chicago.

Knowing that Giuliana is a co-host of the *E! Fashion Police*, I knew I'd have to wear something spectacular to the event, and amazingly, the perfect dress was already in my closet. Just a couple of months earlier, I was surprised with an amazing designer dress I found at a resale shop. Due to being on a tight budget because of disability, I shop at resale shops. I was running errands and stopped by the resale boutique. I happened to see the dress and tried it on. It fit in all the right places, but I couldn't justify buying it because I didn't have an event to wear it to. I left the dress at the store and headed to lunch with my former boss and coworker. I explained through my excitement that, now after having a bilateral mastectomy, I was finally able to wear a dress like this. Prior to my surgery, I had been naturally well endowed, hauling around 34 DDs on my slender, 5'11" frame. This designer dress had a delicate, string, triangle top, which was never an option, pre-surgery. It was silk with beautiful turquoise, fuchsia, and orange splashed across it. It had small, hand-stitched beading reflecting just the right amount of light. It had an asymmetrical hemline making me feel like I left a wake of fabric when I walked. Hours later after our lunch, they surprised me with the dress. At the time, I had no idea where I could wear such a beautiful, one-of-a-kind dress, but I was very appreciative of their gift. And it turned out to be the perfect dress to wear to the *Giuliana and Bill* Season Finale party. I was able to bring a guest, so I brought my best friend, Ashley. We arrived in Chicago, quickly got ready, and met Erica at RPM Italian.

As we entered, we saw dozens of photographers and videographers. We could see Giuliana and Bill being interviewed in one of the booths at the restaurant. There was a deejay who played upbeat songs, providing the soundtrack to the evening. There were servers passing out the couple's favorite drinks, the "Lower Door" with Broker's London Dry Gin, St. Germain, and Cocchi Americano, as well as the "Long-Faced Dove" with Azul Silver Tequila, Campari, Grapefruit, and Ginger Beer. We walked into the bar area of RPM Italian and saw the "step-and-repeat," where celebrities frequently have their picture taken. A wall of ivy and roses with the Style network logo provided the perfect backdrop for photos as we would step, smile, and repeat for the photographers. We took a few quick pictures before the event officially started.

The cameras continued to capture the evening as Giuliana and Bill took the microphone and thanked everyone in attendance. Then, they were in front of the step-and-repeat for the press to take their pictures. Thanks to Erica's connection, I was able to meet them. I noticed Giuliana was also wearing a dress with an asymmetrical hemline, paired with high black heels, and a simple, yet elegant, ponytail. I was aware of her incredibly handsome and charming husband, Bill. Although the moment seemed surreal, I was composed as I briefly shared my connection, my story of infertility and breast cancer with Giuliana. She asked what age and stage I was when originally diagnosed, and then she grabbed Bill's arm and said, "Bill, *listen.*" They fixated on my story since I was diagnosed at a younger age, but originally the same stage as Giuliana. Despite the aggressive treatment I underwent, the cancer still spread to my vital organs. I was aware that my story was her worst nightmare. Knowing that they were expecting via surrogate, my parting words were, "Once you have your child, it will all be worth it." I turned, smiled as a dozen photographers took our picture, and then I disappeared back into the crowd.

While mingling through the crowd, I met another Chicago "It Girl," Lindsay Avner, founder of Bright Pink, which is the only national non-profit organization that focuses on the prevention and early detection of breast and ovarian cancer in young women, while also providing support for high-risk individuals. Lindsay felt like an instant friend who "got it" and focused intently on my story. As we connected, I learned Lindsay was not diagnosed with breast cancer but had an extensive family history of the disease. When she was just 23, she had genetic testing completed and learned she had the gene mutation, which greatly increased her risk of developing breast and ovarian cancer. So, just out of college, Lindsay became the youngest patient to have a prophylactic bilateral mastectomy. Instead of living her life in fear of when she would be diagnosed, she made the decision to have a preventative mastectomy to greatly reduce her risk of the disease. After sharing our stories, we exchanged contact information, and agreed to keep in touch.

Just two months after the Season Finale party, Lindsay connected with me and told me to save the date for October 19, 2012. Lindsay didn't indulge my curiosity and tell me the specifics of the event, but I was looking forward to finding out more.

It turns out Bright Pink was hosting their annual VIPink fundraiser. The event would be held at Saks on Michigan Avenue in Chicago, featuring a fashion show followed by deejays spinning party music.

I was excited about the event and emailed my college girlfriends. I had learned throughout our college years that these girls love a good party, so I wanted to invite them to a party of this magnitude. In my first book, *Learning to Live Legendary*, I described our group of seven and how we connected and bonded during our college years. Each of us had our own unique place in the group. There is Jessi the entrepreneur, Jill the fashionista, Emily the nurse, Lindsay the 'Martha Stewart,' Mollie the athlete, Robin the cheerleader, and me, well, I'd be the planner.

When I extended the invitation, I did it more out of courtesy; I didn't think our group of seven, living everywhere from St. Louis, Missouri to Milwaukee, Wisconsin to Raleigh, North Carolina, would be able to all come together on a Friday night in mid-October. But the power of companionship and connection of this group made it happen.

We reserved a couple of hotel rooms at the Hyatt, just a few of blocks down from Saks. As we got ready, we laughed, caught up, and giggled like we were in college again. It reminded me of our days living in the sorority house together. There were hugs, friendly jabs at one another, and *lots* of laughter. I put on my party dress found at a unique store in Dallas, Texas, and despite having chemotherapy three days earlier, I was ready for a night on the town. We originally connected in college, more than a decade earlier, yet our friendship remained intact despite moving to different areas of the country for jobs and family. I was energized to have my loyal flock of friends to join me for this event; they were the ultimate date I could have for such an occasion.

Word got out that an "unofficial" college reunion was happening, so several other friends from college, residing in Chicago, planned on attending the event. We descended in the hotel elevator and walked in to the lobby bar and saw so many faces from years ago. It had been more than thirteen years since we last saw many of the faces, but they came out to enjoy a reunion and offer their support.

Chicago held true to its nickname of The Windy City. Although we were a few blocks from Saks, we felt the need to start the festivities in grand style, so we arrived in a limo. I was toddling along in five-inch heels, so even though our destination was close, I was grateful for the ride.

We entered the multistory, renowned Saks on Michigan Avenue. The store was closed to general shoppers, but as attendees at this event, we were able to browse and shop. Store attendants were everywhere, offering to help us find that certain something that we just had to have. There must have been a big insurance rider for the event. A mixture of booze, food, and luxurious designer clothing usually doesn't happen, at least not in my world.

We rode the escalator up and heard music pulsing through the air. We arrived on the third floor and saw the set-up for the fashion show. We established our prime position so we could see the models as they gracefully pranced down the runway presenting the latest fashion trends in designer apparel. As the models walked in stilettos, many in our group took off their heels, preferring comfort to fashion. The models continued to strut on the catwalk while we chatted, all seven of us catching up since our last full get-together had been a year and a half ago.

When the fashion show ended, Lindsay Avner, founder of Bright Pink, took the microphone. She spoke of her recent travel to educate others about their program. She shared the story of a woman in her early 20s who found a lump, and after Lindsay's appearance and presentation, the woman made an appointment to have the lump checked out. It turned out the lump was malignant, and not only was cancer in her breast, but it had also spread to other organs in her body.

This event, designed to bring funding to an organization focused on the early detection in young women, just brought a *powerful* voice of awareness to Stage IV breast cancer. The message was clear: Early detection doesn't always save lives. Although age is a risk factor in breast cancer, young women can, and do, get breast cancer.

After an evening of connecting and socializing at the VIPink bash, we headed back to the lobby bar, opting for friends and food over the night clubs that Chicago offers. We created memories as we painted the town red, or pink, because of friendship, not because of cancer.

Infertility makes a person feel alone. Cancer makes a person feel alone. In the end, though, we are not. We are very much connected. I, for example, am connected to Giuliana who was diagnosed with breast cancer after infertility treatment, and I am also connected to all of the women who've likewise been diagnosed—even if their biographies are not publicized. And, the connections with those women are the ones I cherish most.

"The reality of these two enormous losses weighed heavily on me, yet I was careful to conceal my *grief*— choosing to be private in my mourning and not burden others with my emotional misery. I was fiercely *protective* of my family and close friends."

GRIEVING

WHEN I was initially told I had breast cancer, and then again when I was told I had metastatic breast cancer, I grieved, and I moved through the various stages inherent in that process. First there was denial: "This can't happen to me. I'm too young/healthy/ active." Then, anger: "It isn't fair this is happening to me. I was a good person!" Bargaining: "Ok, I'll do all the grueling treatment as long as you promise it won't come back." Next, depression: "I'll never get over this. It's too horrifying." And finally, acceptance: "Cancer. This is my reality." While these stages of grief are common to any life-changing event, they seem to play out more acutely when one's mortality is at stake, and each year, over 211,000 women (and a couple thousand men) move through this grieving process as they are diagnosed with breast cancer. Of those, 211,000, almost 49,000 are diagnosed with metastatic breast cancer each year, and about 40,000 will die annually from metastatic breast cancer. So I found myself grieving in many ways: for myself as well as for the other women I've known, my breast cancer sisters, who have died from the disease.

I remember when I was diagnosed in 2007 that I only knew one other young woman, a coworker, who had been diagnosed with breast cancer. Although she was a coworker, we worked in different departments, so we were merely employees at the same college, not friends. She was a few years older than I was, and when she was diagnosed, it was two years before my own diagnosis. She was the mother of four young boys, ages eight-weeks to eight-years old, at the time of her diagnosis.

Two years later when I was diagnosed, the first email I sent was to her. I still remember exactly where I was when she called, sitting in the office at home, looking for information online. She told me what questions I'd need to ask including if I should get a port: A quarter-sized medical device placed under the skin, just below the collarbone. The port has tubing that goes directly into a central vein leading to the heart. This ensures easy blood draws for labs and doesn't stress the veins in the arm with the toxic chemotherapy. She helped translate the medical jargon of breast cancer. As she talked, I took notes, learning from her experience. She helped make sense out of the nonsense of the disease.

When I was diagnosed Stage IV, this friend was already dealing with her own Stage IV diagnosis, yet she made sure that I had her support. Not only was she my mentor, but she also became a close friend. We'd call each other with results from scans. We'd hole up in the same private chemotherapy room and chat about our precious sons while we each had our chemotherapy infusions. She was able to get into a clinical trial a couple hours away, and I was able to go with her to keep her company. I was the one she called after learning the cancer spread to her brain. I listened on the phone and cried with her as we struggled to digest the most recent information. I watched as she continued on, working full-time, being a mom to four active, young boys, and a wife to a husband with an unpredictable schedule. I sat with her in the hospital as her former students, who were now nurses, cared for her. We found solace in each other, understanding the magnitude of the disease and the implications of its progression to other organs.

When her doctor said her body could no longer handle treatment and she needed to transition to hospice care, I sat in the lobby of the cancer center with her as she cried, mourning her impending death. While she was heavily medicated to help with pain management, I visited her at her home when she was up for it; I sat through visits with the hospice nurse. After she had fallen asleep, I looked her husband straight in the eye and boldly said, "You need to give her permission to die. She is holding on, needing to know the boys will be ok." With tears brimming, he softly replied, "I don't know that I can do that." She lingered on in hospice care for over a month until her body finally gave out, leaving her four children motherless. She was just forty-four years old.

The mental anguish was nearly paralyzing when I attended her funeral. I gazed, almost despondently, at her boys who looked so handsome in their suits. As they individually drifted towards her casket, I wondered if the vision of their mother in a casket would forever be seared into their mind or if they would remember all the times she attended their many sports games, or made them grilled cheeses, or played board games with them. Would they remember her enormous smile and kind laugh? And let's face it: Her funeral also provided an intimate glimpse into my own future when someday my son would be the handsome boy at his own mother's funeral.

Over the past five years, I have lost many friends to this despicable disease, but I've never been so close in proximity as I watched one suffer and succumb to the disease. I was afraid to cry those tears for fear they would not stop, but I did cry at her funeral. Tears ran down my face and fell into my lap as the music "Somewhere Over the Rainbow" by Israel "IZ" Kamakawiwo'ole played. The despair was tangible in my heart, and it was unspeakably agonizing to experience. My mentor and big sister in *cancerland* was now an angel, leaving me with the task to continue mentoring others with the disease. It also left me bearing a distinct, solemn title: Longest living local Stage IV patient.

Then, a week after my mentor died, my mentee was also taken by this disease. I was matched with another young Stage IV breast cancer patient through Imerman Angels. She was just like me, it seemed. She was the same age. She was also divorced. She had young children. And she only lived two hours away.

Our connection began through Imerman Angels, and then we continued to keep in regular contact through emails, talks, and texts. When I registered for the Breast Cancer Recovery Metastatic retreat, I encouraged her to do so as well. She was dealing with significant side effects from treatment and was unable to drive, so I offered to pick her up on the way to the retreat. During our drive, we discussed our remaining treatment options, hopeful at possible clinical trials that could extend our time with our beloved children. She told me the love story of her high school sweetheart re-entering her life after her diagnosis and caring for her and her children while she was in treatment for a terminal diagnosis. At the retreat, we focused on the notion of being "healed even if we aren't cured." But just six months after the conference, her thirty-six-year-old body gave out, leaving her three young children motherless.

The reality of these two enormous losses weighed heavily on me, yet I was careful to conceal my grief—choosing to be private in my mourning and not burden others with my emotional misery. I was fiercely protective of my family and close friends. I didn't want to distress them by confessing my immense grief. They had been with me every step of my own emotional journey, so I tried to protect them from additional heartache. I watched the ravages of cancer, leaving my big sister in *cancerland* looking like a ghost of her former self. I had seen other friends gain weight and retain fluid due to the steroids given as an attempt to subdue the side effects of treatment. Either end of the spectrum left them with a distinct look that did not resemble their former selves.

While I struggled emotionally, physically it was the best I'd felt since my diagnosis. I had energy. I was able to run, well jog really, but I was able to exercise again. Just a year prior, I had such severe side effects from treatment that I struggled to walk up the stairs. As I described earlier, the chemotherapy I was on caused neuropathy. The nerves in my hands were so damaged I struggled to grip and open a water bottle. It was difficult to hold a pen and write decipherable notes on my to-do list. After attending a concert, my friends were fearful that I would get trampled exiting the arena since I had to ascend the stairs so slowly. I kept those struggles concealed to those closest to me in fear that the side effects causing the impairments would be used against me as a single mother. But, a year and two chemotherapies later, physically I felt amazing.

Just days before my routine scan, I learned that another local friend with Stage IV breast cancer died from the disease. This friend was someone I had met in the infusion center. We had chemotherapy on the same days and shared a mutual friend. She was a young wife and intensely private about her disease. She always came to the infusion center by herself, not wanting even her husband to see what she was going through. We frequently saw each other because our chemotherapy schedules aligned. We discussed treatment protocols and clinical trial research in hopes of a cure being found. It was just days before my scan when I got the phone call that she had died at age forty-six. Three young friends had died in under a month's time.

My friend's funeral was, unfortunately, on the same day and at the same time as my next scan, so I was unable to attend. Instead, I mourned in private. Emotionally I was beyond exhausted from maintaining a strong appearance to protect the hearts of others. I lost three friends in less than a month, which was unspeakably agonizing. I also knew the same disease was trying to destroy my own body.

But like I said, I was in a place feeling that I could trust my body. I felt strong. I had energy. I felt "healthy." I was confident going in to my scan, convinced my body was telling me this chemotherapy regime was working. As a Professional Cancer Patient, scans are scheduled every two-three months to confirm if the current treatment is working. Going through scans so frequently begins to feel like playing a game of Russian Roulette—never knowing when the bullet of cancer would launch, showing up in a new area. My scan was the day after Father's Day, and I went to the appointment certain that I would get good results because physically I *felt* healthy.

Often, the time between the scan being completed and getting the results is the most intense emotionally (see "Freaking Out" for specifics). During this period, a radiologist pours over the images, searching for new tumors. My mom and I met with my oncologist that afternoon, just hours after the scan. He entered the room with a somber expression and said, "Well, Jennifer, how are you?" I said, "You have the scan results; you tell me," joking with him. His serious appearance told me this was no time for jokes. The scan revealed the most devastating and damaging results: The cancer had spread to multiple new bones, was now in my liver, and was causing fluid build-up in one lung.

Hot, angry tears streamed down my face. The stages of grief immediately flooded my mind. I was once again betrayed by my body. I felt "healthy"; however, the cancer continued to spread and now invaded a major organ. My oncologist, seeing my anguished panic, said, "This isn't life threatening today. In a year, possibly." While I'm sure he said this to try and be reassuring, I heard the clock of my death start ticking loudly. I never asked for a timeline before and now one was thrust in my lap. *A year.* While rationally I knew that I was already living longer than the average Stage IV patient, I was selfish and wanted more.

I struggled to digest all the information. I was in a dark, horrible place, still trying to process the deaths of three friends in addition to my own devastating news. I fell into a miserable black hole. Still the actress, though, I kept my game face on—especially with those closest to me. I knew that witnessing my emotional pain would only intensify theirs. I knew I needed someone not emotionally invested in my life, so I asked for a referral to a counselor. I chose to grieve and mourn in private in the safety of the counselor's office. Thankfully, I had already asked for additional help . . . better living through chemistry. I continued on the anti-depressant that was prescribed when I was diagnosed Stage IV. At the time of that diagnosis, I told the doctor, "I need something; otherwise I'm going to cry all day, every day." I also asked for help when sleep eluded me. Anxious thoughts about the horrific nature of the disease and watching friends die kept me from sleep. My oncologist agreed with my desire to focus on my quality of life and prescribed a sleeping pill so I could get my brain to turn off when physical exhaustion set in. Our death-denying culture is a place in which no one wants to talk about and acknowledge death, yet it is the reality of the disease and the reality I'm living. Don't get me wrong; although it could be tempting to numb away the pain, the happy pill doesn't make me out of touch with my reality, but it helps me to stay in the "acceptance" phase of grief. Without the help of an anti-depressant and a prescription sleeping pill, I would be a miserable, awful person to be around, and everyone's quality of life would suffer. Without the help, I don't know how I could do something as simple as deleting a dead friend's contact from my phone or my Christmas card list. When I delete the information, it is as if they never existed, yet they had been such an important part of my life. It is also a cruel reminder that one day I will be deleted from someone's contact list, and I can only hope that others will remember me fondly as well.

"A Stage IV cancer diagnosis can turn *strangers* into the most intimate of *friends*."

UNDERSTANDING

BEING diagnosed with cancer at a young age is isolating. It is even more isolating when the disease continues to progress, despite current medical treatments to keep it in remission. There is no cure for breast cancer, as 40,000 women (and a few thousand men) die from the disease each year. Of the women diagnosed with breast cancer, eventually 30% will end up with Stage IV disease. There are currently over 162,000 individuals living with metastatic breast cancer in the United States. While there are plenty of resources for breast cancer survivors and even young women diagnosed with breast cancer, there are relatively few for women with metastatic breast cancer.

One of the few organizations for people like me is The Metastatic Breast Cancer Network (MBCN), which is a national, independent, and non-profit patient advocacy group dedicated to the unique concerns of the women and men living with metastatic breast cancer. MBCN holds an annual conference in a different region of the United States each year, and I have attended two of the last three years.

At the last conference I attended, in October 2012, over 200 women (and a few men) traveled from twenty-two states and two Canadian providences to attend. It happened to be in Chicago. Before each keynote speaker, a patient shared her story, which allowed us to see how others were managing their own Stage IV lives. I was honored when MBCN contacted me and asked me to share my story and speak on the "40 and Under" panel for one of the breakout sessions.

During the opening address, the director of the conference asked everyone diagnosed with metastatic breast cancer to stand. Then she said, "If you were diagnosed less than a year ago, sit down." Over a quarter of the room sat down. "If you were diagnosed less than three years ago, sit down." More than half of the remaining women sat down. The director said, "Those of you still standing, congratulations; you've beaten the odds." People clapped and cheered as if living longer than three years was something to be celebrated! Looking at the handful of remaining women standing, one of my newly diagnosed Stage IV friends, Lorri, asked me, "Well, where are the rest of the long-term survivors? They're just not here (at the conference), right?" If only. While her question was innocent, it was the bold truth. Most of them were not at the conference because they had already died.

The first woman who shared her personal story, right before the first general speaker, became emotional and went on longer than she had been asked to speak. She was filling in for the woman who was scheduled to speak, but who had been hospitalized due to side-effects of treatment. Fearing that I would do the same, the director of the conference found me and reminded me to stay within my allotted five-minute time limit. I told her, "Don't worry; I'm not an emotional speaker. I tend to use inappropriate humor to keep from crying." Later that day, it was my turn, and I walked up to the podium at the Northwestern Lurie Cancer Center auditorium and faced my peers—the only people who could truly understand what it's like to live with Stage IV breast cancer.

This is what I said to them:

"My name is Jen Smith, but you can call me Jay. Since being diagnosed with breast cancer in 2007, I have had both of my breasts and my ovaries removed, so I'm beginning to wonder if I should check the male or female box on questionnaires. I was 30 years-old, nursing my eight month-old son, when I found the lump. At that time, I had a lumpectomy followed by six months of bi-weekly chemo, and seven weeks of daily radiation. After that was done, I was ready to enter the "New Normal" stage that most breast cancer patients talk about—the new normal that includes the horrors of the initial diagnosis and treatment yet looks forward to a return to life and happiness. Instead, just three months after radiation,

I was diagnosed Stage IV with multiple bone metastases. I was 31 and forced to confront my own mortality.

Victoria's Secret may have the million dollar bra, but according to all of the Explanation of Benefits letters I have from my insurance company that list the cost of all of my procedures, I have the million dollar body. In the past five years, I've had two lumpectomies, an oopherectomy, a bilateral mastectomy, 17 different treatments (anti-hormonal, chemotherapy, targeted therapy), and radiation to six areas of my body. Despite this, the cancer has continued to spread to numerous new bones and my liver. It's funny, though, because as my body has become more scarred and mutilated, my spirit and sense of self-worth has become stronger—more empowered. I realize now that the body is just a vessel—full of imperfections. It succumbs to cancer. It isn't as strong and powerful as we'd like to believe. What is important is what the vessel holds; what it holds is sublime and transcendent.

Just like you, I've faced challenges and fears, and my biggest fear is that my son won't remember me, and our special bond, if I succumb to this disease. Note, I didn't say "sickness" because that would imply that I'm contagious or I'm sick and will get better. As much as I believe in miracles, I also know the cruel reality of this disease. Cancer is a thief and murderer—not a "sickness."

I've become a hospital hussy, going for second opinions in St. Louis, Houston, Chicago, and Indianapolis in search of answers, hoping to meet my dream man, "NED." Hearing there is No Evidence of Disease (NED) of cancer in your body is like finding the

Holy Grail. For some people, it comes easily . . . for others, like me, it doesn't come so easily or at all, no matter how hard we try. We stalk NED incessantly—yet never quite find him. When I was diagnosed Stage IV, I knew there was no Stage V, so I decided to consider myself in Stage Thrive. I decided to focus on my QUALITY of life since my quantity would likely be compromised. So how did I do this? I got out of a bad marriage. I made goals . . . my son was almost two at the time of my Stage IV diagnosis, and my goal became to see him go to kindergarten, which just happened in August, 2012. When statistically I should have been dead, I left my dream job as an academic advisor and instead of focusing on dying, I decided to make a bucket list to accomplish my greatest dreams. What unfolded became known as the Magic 7 of 2011. When I accomplished those goals, I wrote my memoir, *Learning to Live Legendary* because what's the point in living unless it's legendary! And I am honored to be here among so many other legendary people."

The audience understood my longing for NED while going through never-ending, or palliative, treatment. The audience warmly welcomed the speaker I was honored to introduce, Dr. Patricia Steeg. Dr. Steeg connected with the group and discussed how her research team was investigating ways to prevent breast cancer from spreading to the brain. She was also very candid in explaining how our current clinical trial system works, the flaws in the system, and the need to think outside the box. Her presentation was enlightening, but she also presented at the patient level so we were able to clearly understand why there aren't giant breakthroughs in research offering the elusive cure each of us desperately seeks.

After Dr. Steeg's lecture, the "40 and Under" breakout session occurred. A room with more than fifty women diagnosed under the age of 40 discussed the distinct differences and challenges of being diagnosed at such a young age. I was included among the four panelists, but it turned into a group discussion as we understood each other on so many different levels. Recommendations for second opinions, suggestions for treatment-related side effects, and discussion of treatment protocols were shared–in the hopes that someone else could benefit from the information.

A few of us from the "40 and Under" breakout session connected and lingered at a table after the session. The conversation drifted to the inevitable: Death from this disease—the really dark place that accompanies a Stage IV diagnosis. One of the young women said she felt like a burden to her family. Another shared her anxiety over the cost of her treatment and its impact on her family's finances. Of course, even more challenging is the emotional toll of a diagnosis of this magnitude. Young wives wondered if their spouses would remarry and what kind of person they'd want their spouse to search for. Young mothers confessed how unsettling it is to think of another woman raising her children after her anticipated death. Another young woman questioned if her spouse was staying with her just because she has cancer. I engaged in a conversation with another young, single woman, and we debated over whether it is "fair" to date and potentially fall in love with a person, knowing that our own death would cause extensive grief to our partner. Our group discussed the feelings of immense loss for the end of a beautiful friendship when one of our peers dies, but appreciation for an understanding in a way that most couldn't begin to comprehend. We shared the raw emotion of sheer terror watching a loved one die of the same disease attacking our own bodies. There was a lot of talk that revolved around our friends who had been stolen by this disease and the feelings of guilt for outliving them, especially if they were diagnosed more recently than we had been. Cancer just isn't logical, we agreed, and each diagnosis, treatment plan, and ultimate death runs according to its unique chronology.

Although she wasn't at the conference, a recent conversation with my friend Reesa, also Stage IV, flooded my brain. Reesa was diagnosed Stage IV two years after me. When the cancer in her body progressed from her bones to her liver, she simply said, "Well, Jen: I trumped you." While it may sound cold and morbid, I understood exactly what she meant: The cancer in her body continued to ravage a vital organ in addition to her bones, while, on the other hand, mine, at the time, remained in my bones. With her comment, there was also an overtone of jealousy, as my quality of life was fairly good at the time while hers was clearly not.

While our group sat discussing death and dying, a woman who appeared to be old enough to be the mother to any of us approached the table and joined the conversation. She had the bragging-rights at the conference; she had been living with Stage IV cancer for 12 years. Many of us young adults long to reach her age and be the one to strut and proudly say how long we've lived with a terminal diagnosis. While I would think she would know better, she gave the empty advice that society has conditioned us to offer. "Be strong." "Stay positive." "It will all be OK."

One of the young women at the table, Jennie, challenged this. She said, "But, it's not OK. My good friend who was my roommate at this conference last year died in January. She was 32." Others chimed in, "It's not okay that my toddler may have no memory of me." "It's not okay that cancer robbed me of my fertility, and I cannot have children." "It's not ok that my child will have to learn the brutal reality of this disease when he learns the treatment has stopped working, and my death is impending, and he will grow up without his mommy," I nearly shouted. The empty advice from the older woman dishonored not only those of us living with the disease, but also those who have died from the disease.

While the intention wasn't to attack the woman who joined the conversation, it did serve as a reality check to the well-meaning, yet misguided, comments that people often offer in attempt to be supportive. A simple, "I'm sorry you're going through this," is truly all that needs to be said.

A Stage IV cancer diagnosis can turn strangers into the most intimate of friends. These friends that I've made truly understand my journey, and I truly understand theirs. And while I am terrified of losing them to the same disease that is killing me, I still love them and draw them yet closer to me. These people, some of whom are still alive and some of whom have now died, have alleviated the sense of isolation that a Stage IV cancer diagnosis brings, and I am forever grateful for their unconditional love, understanding, and support.

"The word *believe* became a subconscious mantra as I continued on in treatment for Stage IV *breast cancer.*"

BELIEVING

WHEN the scans showed the breast cancer returned and spread to multiple bones, I panicked. A Stage IV diagnosis comes with an expiration date; average life expectancy is less than three years. When I was diagnosed Stage IV, my nightmare became my reality. My son, Corbin, was almost two and I desperately wanted to watch him grow up and make special memories with him. With the new Stage IV diagnosis, I felt an urgent need to start making those special memories *immediately*, so I decided I wanted to take Corbin to Disney World while I was still in relatively good health. At the time of my Stage IV diagnosis, I watched a friend go from Stage IV diagnosis to death in a mere nine months. I knew that the disease was unpredictable and aggressive treatment was needed in hopes of extending my life. I also realized that if I only had nine months, like my friend, I needed to be vigilant in how I spent my remaining time.

When I started planning the trip to Disney World, I was still married to Corbin's father. As I continued planning, my marriage imploded, and headed to divorce. The divorce almost diverted my efforts in planning the trip due to financial strain and sheer emotional exhaustion. Thankfully, I learned about Memories of Love, a nonprofit organization that sends a patient with a life-threatening diagnosis, and their family, to Orlando for a vacation. Since I did not have a spouse, my sister, Sara, was able to join Corbin, who was two-and-a-half at the time, and me as my "caregiver" for part of the trip. This trip happened over Mother's Day weekend in 2009.

The first day in Orlando, we drove our rental car to the Disney World parking lot. We climbed aboard the tram and rode it to the monorail station. When we started to exit the tram, Corbin started to cry, thinking it was a ride. Thankfully we were able to distract him by showing him the space-age-looking monorail. We sat in the front car of the monorail with a clear view all around and watched as we approached Magic Kingdom. It seemed as if we were gliding through air as the castle became closer. As we entered the gates and felt the magic of Mickey Mouse in the air, I knew those enchanting memories were being formed.

Just one ride into our vacation a crazy accident happened. We were getting in line for the flying Dumbo ride. Just outside the entrance, there was a photo opportunity with a replica of the Dumbo ride. I quickly took a picture of Sara and Corbin "riding" on Dumbo, and then we swapped places. After Sara took our picture, I picked up Corbin to exit. I thought the stairs down from the photo opportunity went straight out from Dumbo, and since I was carrying Corbin, I couldn't see that the stairs actually wrapped around to the side. I stepped off the first platform, and my heel caught on the way down, badly twisting my ankle. With the momentum, Corbin launched from my arms and I watched in sheer terror as he hit the cement. Time seemed to be in fragments as I saw my baby, my only child, airborn, and cold, hard, mauve pavement below him. My sister came running over and was able to console Corbin who seemed startled but wasn't injured. I remained on the ground with searing pain in my ankle. A stranger approached and asked if I was okay. Through my tears I said, "No," so he ran and got a Disney staff member who alerted the medical team. We were only one hour into our vacation, and I was afraid our memories were going to include a trip to the Emergency Department.

The medical team arrived quickly and assessed the situation. I remained on the pavement; my concern was for Corbin to be assessed first. After they evaluated Corbin, I was able to stand with help and put light pressure on my ankle. One employee, named Brendan, asked basic questions, including where we were from. I told him we were from Illinois, and he responded he went to school in Illinois, and we discovered we went to the same university for undergraduate school. The pain was subsiding, and as I realized this bizarre connection, I started to laugh and told him, "My family teases me that we can't go anywhere without running into someone I know." Although we attended college at different times, it was such a coincidence that we met several thousand miles away at Disney World. In further talking to him, he also mentioned that his wife had breast cancer at a young age. I was completely amazed at the similarities.

Thankfully, my ankle wasn't seriously injured. After a bit of time, I was able to walk without issue. I asked my sister to take a picture of me with Brendan for my scrapbook of memories when we returned home. While I'm smiling in the picture, the top of my head is cut off and Brendan has a look of alarm because Sara started to faint while taking the picture. My sister is an athlete who works out regularly and has run several marathons, so seeing her start to collapse was shocking. The paramedics were able to get her to a shaded area and took her blood pressure and other vitals. It turns out the adrenaline that supported her getting me through my crisis was now gone, leaving her wobbly. I snapped a picture of the medics attending to her that happens to have a Disney logo with "A Lifetime of Vacation Memories" sign in the background. I'm guessing most Disney World guests don't have those kinds of memories! I was relieved that after a few minutes in the shade, she was just fine and we *finally* got in line for the Dumbo ride. We completely covered Magic Kingdom and were able to go on all the rides Corbin wanted to try. Over the next several days, we went to Animal Kingdom and Sea World, all without incident.

My sister had to fly out a day before we did at the end of our vacation. After we dropped her off at the airport, Corbin and I headed to Downtown Disney. This boardwalk area has a vast collection of shops, restaurants, and Disney World memorabilia. While in one shop, Corbin saw a magnet he wanted to get as a gift for my dad. The magnet was a guitar, a fitting tribute to my dad who plays bass guitar. While looking at the magnets, I saw a pewter angel. Engraved on the wings of the angel it simply said, "Miracles happen, just believe." I decided that we would get the magnets as a remembrance of this special trip. After a Stage IV diagnosis, divorce, and injury at Disney, it truly was a miracle that Corbin and I were standing in this shop. The magnet seemed so fitting for everything we'd been through.

The angel magnet was the first one I placed on my refrigerator as Corbin and I moved into our new home, after the divorce. I also found a large wooden sign that says "BELIEVE: Now faith is being sure of what we hope for and certain of what we do not see. Hebrews 11:1." I hung the sign on the hallway wall connecting my bedroom to Corbin's. The word *believe* became a subconscious mantra as I continued on in treatment for Stage IV breast cancer.

As I completed the goal of taking Corbin to Disney World, I made a bigger goal: See him go to kindergarten. Statistically this goal was improbable, yet I clung to the word: *believe*. I found myself continually thinking back to the magnet. Seeing Corbin start kindergarten would indeed be an utter miracle. As the months continued on to years of living with Stage IV breast cancer, this phenomenal dream became a reality, and I knew I wanted to do something bold and memorable in honor of the special day.

While many associate the idea of a tattoo with impulsive and immature behavior, I wanted a permanent memento of reaching this seemingly unrealistic, yet miraculous, goal. I decided to make my mantra a permanent part of my body, just like the many scars I have from surgeries. For me, it was a powerful, and permanent, way to reclaim my body. It was a way of "marking my territory" after the many scars from surgery had marked theirs. I had the word *believe* tattooed on the inside of my left wrist. I wanted it in a prominent location, where I would often see it. There were many dark and raw moments where I didn't believe I would see this day. I knew that I needed this permanent reminder of the saying on the magnet, "Miracles happen, just *believe*." Although I attend church regularly, I don't consider myself a religious person, but I do have a very strong faith. The word believe tapped into my spiritual side, but also was a bold reminder in times when I didn't *believe* I would see my miracle happen.

I spent hours exploring font options, researching local tattoo parlors, and learning of other's experiences. In the end, everything led to an upscale, clean, tattoo shop aptly named No Regrets. Instead of using a font found online, I used a truly unique one: Corbin's own handwriting. I had him write "believe" over a dozen times. In true five-year-old penmanship, there wasn't one that was entirely legible. So, like a puzzle, I pieced together different letters from the collection to obtain the perfect font.

I thought of getting the tattoo on Corbin's first day of kindergarten, but I knew the day would already be full of adrenaline pumping activities. Instead, I decided to get the tattoo a few weeks earlier on an equally significant date, my nephew's first birthday. Maybe the tradition started when I got my ears pierced on my 10th birthday, but if I was going to permanently alter my body by choice and not by medical necessity, I wanted the date to be significant. Thankfully, my sister was able to join me and take pictures while I grimaced as the needle punctured my skin with black dye. The whole procedure lasted less than five minutes and (thankfully) the pain ended as soon as the tattoo artist was done. Now, I had a permanent commemoration of the miracle about to happen, Corbin starting kindergarten.

It wasn't my first or my last tattoo, which may be a surprise. I'm not artsy or impulsive. I've led a pretty predictable, planned life. My first tattoo, a cross with a pink ribbon hanging on it, was inked on my left foot on the one-year anniversary of my first surgery. The tattoo was a permanent reminder that I could not have gotten through the struggles of a breast cancer diagnosis without my faith. The tattoo was to be a celebration of reclaiming my body and being "cancer free" for a year. Only two weeks later, we learned of the recurrence and tumors in multiple bones. Maybe the cruel irony of timing was to remind me that my faith sustains me as I continued on in treatment. I truly believe that without my faith, I would not be at peace with where I am in life.

My trend of choosing to make my own mark on my body on a significant date continued; my five year "cancerversary." Every person diagnosed with cancer can tell you the date of their diagnosis.

September 7, 2007. I was in an exam room at the radiologist's office, still in my hospital gown. The incision from my biopsy hadn't healed because my body was still producing breast milk which leaked through the incision. The radiologist requested a return appointment to make sure there wasn't a hematoma or infection at the biopsy site. After he examined the site and told me it looked fine, he left the room. Then he re-entered and said, "The pathology is back, and I'm sorry to say it shows cancer." At that moment, the room went quiet as tears began to spill down my cheeks. One of the techs asked if there was anyone I could call. My former husband was out of state, but thankfully my mom worked at the hospital. I called her bawling and could only mumble, "It's cancer," through my heaving sobs. Her reply was panicked, "Where are you? I want to be with you," and ran through the halls. In hindsight, news of this magnitude should never be given to a patient who is alone.

My mom arrived in the exam room and after a long hug and many tears, we went and met with my nurse practitioner. She was the health professional I first saw when I found the lump. She had repeatedly said, "I'm sure it's nothing, but let's have it looked at just to be sure." Now she had a look of shock, and her expression was pure sorrow. We now had evidence that indeed it was something. We asked some basic questions, and she gave me the first of many appointments at the Carle Cancer Center.

At that first appointment, my oncologist said, "If you complete surgery, the recommended six months of aggressive chemotherapy, and seven weeks of daily radiation, you'll have an 85% chance of being cancer-free in five years." I was appalled, over the diagnosis in general, but also over that statistic! I was an over-achiever in school, and in the last two years of undergraduate and all of graduate school, I only earned one "B." This 85% wasn't a number I was familiar with! What about the message often preached that "early detection saves lives"? I was thirty-years young with a ten-month old baby at home. I struggled to comprehend what this meant, I couldn't believe this was my reality.

Then, when I drove home from the appointment, I shifted my thinking. "Well, if someone told me I had an 85% chance at winning the lottery, I'd starting thinking of what I'd do with the money. I'd focus on what I could spend that money on rather than worry about the 15% chance that I wouldn't win." This revelation helped set my outlook for the future. I'm also a visual person and my mom made me a special chart, a calendar that started with the year I was born. She colored each month a different bright color, then during the time I'd be in treatment, she colored it gray. After treatment ended, she continued to color each month with bright colors, extending all the way to my 80th birthday. This calendar was a visual representation to help me realize how little time treatment for cancer would play in my entire lifespan.

Just three months after treatment ended, we learned the gray would continue on, muting the dazzling colors on the calendar. The doctors explained that the cancer had returned, despite the fact I completed an incredibly aggressive treatment plan. Not only had it returned; it had spread to multiple bones, making it a terminal diagnosis. Once a patient is diagnosed with Stage IV cancer, they are in treatment for the rest of their life, which is greatly shortened due to the aggressive nature of the disease. The average life expectancy is less than three years. At the age of 31, I was forced to truly confront the illusion of immortality. Breast cancer wasn't going to be a gray past; it was going to be part of every day in my future.

Early stage breast cancer patients talk about their "new normal" of life after cancer. My "new normal" was going to include being on some kind of treatment for the rest of my life. And my life that my mom projected out to 80+ years was significantly reduced. I tried to wrap my brain around this information; however, it seemed impossible, I couldn't believe it. Seeing a future with continual doctor's appointments, frequent scans, and constant treatment was looking very depressing.

As I realized my future would be greatly condensed, I struggled to *believe*. The bright colors of the chart my mom made seemed to disintegrate. It would be unlikely I'd see my 40th birthday, let alone my 80th. So I decided to focus on my *quality* of life since my quantity of life, would be compromised due to this disease. When I decided to focus on my quality of life it became clear I needed to eliminate drama and unnecessary stress, and instead focus on the value of true friendships. I started to *believe* as I realized how amazing it is that God will place people in your life when you least expect it. Thankfully, on my fifth cancerversary, five full years from the date of my diagnosis, I was able to celebrate it with someone who came into my life *after* my Stage IV diagnosis. I flew to Dallas for the weekend and spent time with my best friend, Ashley.

We originally met at an Illini football game in the fall of 2009. At that time, we lived in the same neighborhood, less than 100 yards from one another. As our friendship grew, we remembered we had briefly met years earlier as we were both on a search committee for a volleyball coach at Parkland College. She was the student athlete representative, I was the EEO committee member. There were many differences between Ashley and me. She is eight years younger. She hasn't been married, had a child, been through a divorce, or a diagnosis of breast cancer. She has long blonde hair, while I have a short, dark pixie cut. Her favorite clothes were dresses, while I preferred jeans and a t-shirt. Although there were many differences, our friendship grew into a tight bond. We went on walk-and-talks. As we walked through the neighborhood, the nearby golf course, and the cornfields we lived near, we helped each other through heartbreaks, job dilemmas, and devastating health news. Although Ashley is eight years younger, her self-confidence, integrity, and maturity helped me grow and realize my true love for myself. We spent time hosting "girls night in" and watched various award shows as we became our own version of the fashion police. We swam in her pool while we watched Corbin create assorted dives and gave him scores for his brilliant and hilarious imagination.

Ashley was my go-to person. After I had several headaches for a few days, I scheduled a brain MRI to see if the cancer had spread. I didn't want to alarm my family, so Ashley came over and stayed with Corbin while I went to my scan. She was also my go-to person for fun; I often "shopped" in her closet for a new dress to wear out. She was also my travel partner: Hawaii, Indianapolis, Pittsburgh, Chicago, and Cancun, to name a few. And, while one person actually questioned, and I'm sure several more have wondered, she's not *that kind* of partner; we're both straight. For some reason, two tall, attractive women who enjoy spending time together apparently raise that question.

When my go-to person, my best friend, and confidant moved to Dallas for a job, I worried that our bond would decrease as the miles between us increased. I knew my five-year cancerversary had to be spent with her. I knew she recognized the significance of this milestone. I also knew there wouldn't be any false pretense of what my life is truly like.

I arrived in Dallas and was greeted by Ashley in typical girl fashion: Squeals, jumping up and down, and hugs. We went to her new condo, and I put down my suitcase. I reviewed messages on my phone as I walked back into her kitchen. She said, "Ohhh, I'm nervous, I feel like I'm about to propose." That got my attention as my curiosity skyrocketed! She then calmly said, "I'm going to get a tattoo." My immediate reply was, "Does your mom know about this?!" (due to our previous shenanigans that raised some questions from her family). I didn't want to be seen as the bad influence since I already had two tattoos. She said, "Yes, she knows. I decided that I want to do something in honor, not in memory, of you. Even though I've moved to Texas, I want you to know that I will forever be your best friend." She went on to explain she wanted the word *forever* tattooed on her rib cage. I loved the idea behind it and told her I wanted to get it too. I joked that it's the grown up, permanent version of the BFF necklace young girls wear.

We headed to a reputable tattoo parlor (thankfully she'd done her research) and got inked up. The tattoo is written in a beautiful script and is discrete. Mine is covered when wearing a bikini. Yep, even though I don't have breasts, I still wear a bikini. This was the perfect way to celebrate our friendship and commemorate my five-year cancerversary, which at one point I didn't believe I'd reach.

I have nearly two feet of scars from multiple surgeries required for treatment of metastatic breast cancer. I have also electively altered my body: *believe, forever,* and a cross with a pink ribbon hanging on it. Choosing to alter my body and reclaim it, on my terms, not cancer's, has helped me believe that I'm in control. While I cling to the word *believe,* I don't mean to imply that it is that simple and that is why I'm still alive. That would suggest that I have some innate drive that others have lacked when their lives have been stolen by the vile disease of Stage IV breast cancer. I know that is not true, but that powerful expression engraved on the magnet on the angel's wing "Miracles happen, just believe" has been my focal point in learning to live with Stage IV breast cancer.

"Since being diagnosed with *terminal* breast cancer, I can find a reason to *celebrate* just about anything."

CELEBRATING

BIRTHDAYS: oh, how I wish I could have more. I'd gladly take on more wrinkles, a few extra pounds, and some gray hair for more of them. I wouldn't dread them. I wouldn't hide them from friends and family and refuse to tell others my age. I would shout it out: I'm 40 . . . I'm 50 . . . I'm 80 amazing years-old! Why is it that we don't really value age? In our search for eternal youth, we overlook the great gifts of age: Like time, like experience, like wisdom.

When I turned 35 in 2012, I was surprised to still be alive, so I decided to scrap my birth *day* and celebrate my birth *month* with the theme: "I'm 35 and Still Alive!" I was well aware that I was on borrowed time, and that if this birthday was going to be my last, I wanted it to be celebrated with all those I hold dear to me, so I carefully planned as many lunches, dinners, and get-togethers as I could during the month of March.

I was able to celebrate my 35th birthday with my family at my favorite restaurant, Biaggi's. I was able to celebrate my birthday with my girlfriends from college with a weekend getaway in Raleigh, North Carolina. And I was able to celebrate my birthday with my best friend, Ashley, with dinner and a night of festivities to celebrate getting older. Each of these times, we celebrated with dessert. We also celebrated with deep appreciation for the time we had together. Joy and love surrounded us. But, even as I celebrated, I struggled. Would this be my last birthday? Would they continue to celebrate my birthday after cancer has killed me? Would I celebrate another birthday, not just of mine, but what about my family members'?

Part of who I am wants to celebrate the accomplishments, victories, and small moments for others as well. In 2012, I wasn't the only one celebrating: My mom celebrated turning 60. To commemorate her birthday, our family had a weekend getaway in Chicago. While we frequent the city on a regular basis, this trip was special. We stayed at the Palmer House in downtown Chicago. My late grandparents, my mom's parents, stayed there for their honeymoon. The lobby atmosphere has old school charm and magnificent beauty. As we stood in the lobby, I had a surreal feeling knowing that my grandparents had once walked on the same beautiful marble floors. I felt at peace knowing I was celebrating an age I wouldn't reach. I was able to appreciate that my mom had celebrated her life by watching her children grow-up and meeting her grandchildren.

Another epic birthday happened in the summer of 2012, when my nephew, Jaxson, turned one. While this is certainly a milestone birthday for all babies, I was so thrilled I got to celebrate with him. My brother, Jaxson's father, got engaged a couple of months after my Stage IV diagnosis in 2009. At that time, the only friend I lost to breast cancer went from Stage IV diagnosis to death in nine months. My brother's engagement was nine months long, and I desperately wanted to be at the wedding. Thankfully, I was able to celebrate their marriage, and then two years later learned they were expecting! Getting to see my brother and sister-in-law go through pregnancy, and a six week early delivery, was the closest I would ever be to "being" pregnant again.

It was a great struggle to get pregnant with my own son, Corbin. I loved being pregnant and even considered being a surrogate just to experience bringing another life into this world. A breast cancer diagnosis and the required treatment completely destroyed my dreams of having more children.

I loved meeting my nephew, but in the back of my mind, I wondered if he would remember me when this disease steals me from his life. I wondered if I'll get to meet future nieces and nephews. While I focus so much love on my son, I also adore celebrating and loving my nephew. Corbin is almost five years older, so I'd forgotten how I celebrated all those little firsts: Rolling, crawling, walking, talking, and more. Watching my nephew, Jaxson, accomplish those firsts, I was reminded to celebrate the everyday miracles that happen all around us.

There is much to celebrate in life. And while most might agree that big moments like a graduation, a wedding, or the birth of a child are worthy of celebration, not all might recognize the small moments as worthy of such as well. But I think we deserve . . . no, we *must*, celebrate the little moments too.

Since being diagnosed with terminal breast cancer, I can find a reason to celebrate just about anything. It's a beautiful, sunny day? Let's get ice cream, and then let's go play at the park. It's a dreary snow-covered winter day? Let's built a fort out of blankets, and then watch our favorite movie. I appreciate being present as the seasons change. While others may dread helping their child with homework, I am grateful that I am still alive and helping him as he learns. I want to be here and deal with him as a surly teenager. And while death is lingering in the back of my mind, I realize that no one knows when their expiration date truly is, so I encourage you to appreciate the small accomplishments that often seem mundane. Take a moment to stop and realize the gift of life rather than continually being caught up in the chaos of now.

While some view their birthday as "just another day," I truly hope people are encouraged to *celebrate* their special day. Celebrations can happen in grand fashion or can be as simple as taking the day off of work to treat yourself and enjoy spending time doing something you are completely passionate about. Instead of being preoccupied with gifts and things, I want to challenge you to celebrate simply being alive and turning another year older. Take the time to celebrate you. And take the time to celebrate all of those little moments in between.

"And while my family has given me many gifts—laughter, memories, and support—the biggest gift I can give them is permission, the *ultimate gift* of permission to go on loving, laughing, and living despite *grieving*."

COPING

MY family grew up middle-class in central Illinois. While most people associate Chicago with the state of Illinois, we grew up in Champaign, about 2½ hours south. While surrounded by cornfields, the city of Champaign is home to the world-renowned University of Illinois, Parkland College, Ebertfest, and the Illinois Marathon. Champaign is also home to several Fortune 500 companies. Multiple Olympic athletes, a two-time winner of the Nobel Prize in Physics, the co-founders of YouTube, professional athletes, authors, and musicians have called Champaign "home" at one point in their lives.

We moved to Champaign when I was five, for my father's career in agriculture research. My mom was a labor and delivery nurse at the local hospital and now works on the administration side of the Neonatal Intensive Care Unit. We did not struggle financially, but we also did not have a lavish lifestyle growing up. My parents were able to provide well beyond our "needs" and into our "wants," but they taught us the value of living within our means. They carefully instilled a good work ethic in us, not wanting us to have a feeling of entitlement. Often, instead of giving us trendy material things, my parents gave us memories.

When I was a child, my family would go on a summer vacation each year. One year we drove to the Colorado Rockies and Utah Arches National Park. We spent our time hiking and exploring the mountains. Our family, always up for teasing and fun, would jump out and scare one another from behind a tree or boulder. One summer, we were visiting prospective colleges for my brother. After a long day of driving and exploring the campus, we were all hungry, so we packed up the minivan to go to the hotel. As we crossed the bridge over the interstate, my dad made a left turn. "Holy balls, we're on the interstate again!" rushed out of his mouth as we all struggled not to respond to his frustration by giggling at the absurd phrase. At the time, we knew not to react to his outburst, but all these years later, we still tease him about his "holy balls" wording choice. Another year, we drove to Washington D.C. and went to the Smithsonian Museum and other national landmarks. Our trips, however, weren't always distant locations; one year we went to Door County, Wisconsin. We camped in a log cabin, hiked, and swam in the lake. When we went to Wisconsin, I had just received my driver's license, and to my surprise, my parents let me rent a scooter. My dad and I went on our own tour of the wooded forest. I felt an incredible sense of independence as I cruised along on the scooter. I joked that I was going to buy a shirt for my brother that said, "Don't worry, I'm just her brother" since my adolescent identity was noticing all the young men around and I didn't want them to perceive my brother as my boyfriend.

We grew up in a comfortable home with a large backyard connected to a commons area full of grass, creeks, and walking paths. When it rained, the commons area flooded, and we would get out a canoe and paddle around the "pond." We were in a neighborhood bursting with other children our age. During summer evenings at dusk, we often played ghosts in the graveyard or caught fireflies.

We also had typical family issues. My brother, three years younger, and I fought a lot—common, of course, in sibling relationships. My sister, who is six years younger, avoided conflict and was often the peacekeeper; she got along with both of us. As we matured, we grew into friends. We realized our parents' rules were made and enforced out of love and were not an attempt to make us miserable.

I continued along the path I had always envisioned for my future. I went to college, fell in love, began a career, got married, and had a baby. I saw life's events as one big to-do list and went about checking off the major milestones. I thought little about the day-to-day moments and focused on the next "task" to complete. Since my diagnosis and divorce, much has changed. My to-do list is focused on being a mom and trying to stay alive.

After my divorce, I became a single mother, and I'm grateful for all that my parents do to help me. In a way, they fill in as my missing spouse. For example, if I'm running late from a chemotherapy appointment, one of my parents picks up Corbin from school. Or, if I'm giving a presentation or attending a meeting in the evening, my parents come to my house, watch my son, and put him to bed. They come to open houses and holiday concerts at his school. Because of this intimacy, Corbin has an incredible bond with Mamoo, or my mom, and Papa.

When I was growing up, my extended family lived in Ohio, so we only saw them a few times a year. Now, since my immediate family all lives in the same town, we have near-weekly dinners together. We truly enjoy each other's company and spend time hanging out at each other's homes. Spending time together has given us plenty of memories and endless material for inside jokes and reasons to tease one another. They still, in fact, give me a hard time about a comment I made on that family trip to Colorado. Prior to the trip, I had, of course, seen pictures of mountains, but as we drove closer to the Rocky Mountain range, I couldn't fathom how tall they were. I could tell the distance between the minivan and the base of the mountain, so I said, "I know they couldn't, but if they did fall over, would the mountains squish us?" As a teen from central Illinois, I was simply trying to grasp the enormity of the mountains. I wasn't trying to be a daft teen. Growing up in the land of cornfields, where I could see for miles on the horizon, I was struggling to take in being able to see miles vertically. My family, however, found my question prime material for teasing. Twenty years later, they still tease me about mountains falling over, and we still tease my dad about his "holy balls" outburst.

Our family is great at making memories and tends to thrive on humor, especially during difficult and emotional times. We weren't, however, great at talking about deep emotional and personal feelings. And, something like a cancer diagnosis doesn't necessarily force a family to change the way it functions. It takes deliberate, intentional effort in communication to make those changes.

Since my diagnosis, I have wanted to protect my family and loved ones, so I attempted to keep my grief private. My family, in fact, functions much the same way. But in my attempt to really reveal what happens when someone is diagnosed with terminal breast cancer, I asked my father to candidly tell me how he deals with the stress of my situation. This is what my dad wrote about how he shows his love through acts of service:

The medical issues leave me feeling overwhelmed and totally out of my element, so I am very grateful that Mom is able to help with that. My first inclination is to try and "fix" things, so I guess I try and fill that role whenever there is a chance. I can't do much, but when I insulate your windows, put on a storm door, or help with Corbin, it's my way of trying to be supportive, even when I'm not at the doctor's appointments.

More than my hair color has changed over the last five years. I haven't yet conquered worry and fear, but worry and fear leading to a lot of prayer has deepened my faith and trust in God. I have tried to stop demanding answers or action and instead try to be truly thankful for every small blessing and every moment we are allowed to share as a family, even moments like when Corbin threw up all over me at Disney World.

Looking back, I am sure that I have not processed feelings and emotions the right way. Some of the people at work, and some innocent strangers, have had to see pent-up anger appear out of nowhere. God and I are working on it. I don't know if the partial success has come from my praying for it or from others praying for me. I guess I need to try and remember: There are a lot of people, many of whom we will never know, praying especially for you, but also for the whole family. That is pretty awesome, if we will just recognize and accept it.

My mom, on the other hand, shows her love through quality time: Attending every doctor's appointment and chemotherapy infusions I've had. When asked how she deals with my diagnosis, she wrote this:

You have said that your cancer diagnosis has to be a parent's worst nightmare, and I would agree. It has been very difficult from the beginning, but especially after your Stage IV diagnosis. As a mother, every cell of me is programmed to protect and take care of my children, no matter their age. I want to make things all better. I have wished so many times that I could take your place. The feelings of lack of control and helplessness can be overwhelming at times. Coming to your appointments and treatments is a very small way that I can feel like I'm doing something. I hope that I am a source of strength and comfort for you, and I will always be there.

"Faith, family, and friends" really sums up what has helped me during the past five years. I know that God has His hand in our lives and this journey, although we may question it and don't always understand His plan. And I know that many family members and friends are praying for me and our family as well as for you. They are my prayer warriors and a source of strength and comfort.

A friend and former neighbor, who lost her 24 year-old daughter to lung cancer, sent a card to your dad and me when you were first diagnosed, saying that they were praying for us. Then she said, 'May God bless you all as you learn to appreciate the good days and strengthen you for the difficult ones.' I have carried that blessing in my heart. I think this experience has helped our whole family to more fully appreciate all the blessings we have been given.

Another friend once said, 'I'm sure it's the first thing you think of every day and the last thing you think of every night.' And she is right—you are in my prayers as I wake and when I go to sleep. Your disease is like a shadow . . . it is always with me, but more apparent at times. On the good days, the lines between light and dark are sharp, the disease is contained, and life is appreciated and enjoyed. But on the dark days, the shadow lines blur with grayness, and it spreads. My hope and desire is to help bring light into your days and to be with you in the gray ones.

One of the hardest times for me (and obviously for you) is the time around scans to see if treatment is working or the disease has spread. I have learned that I am more tense, distracted, and irritable at these times. Recognizing the source of my tension was a first step. I have found prayer/quiet time, family time, and exercise all help—somewhat.

The biggest thing that has helped me during this journey is YOU. I remember you saying that you couldn't control the fact that you have this disease but that you can control your response to it and you have certainly done that! I am in awe of your ability to face this disease head on; to show grace and strength and faith while confronting your own mortality; and to help so many women who are fighting this disease by advocating for them, planning conferences, speaking, and writing.

And then there's my dear sister, Sara. Although she is six years younger, she has incredible insight. In asking my sister how she has coped during the past five years, she wrote this:

I think we have been very fortunate in seeing how you have dealt with everything and have been able to follow your lead. Our family has seemed to settle into a similar response of allowing ourselves to grieve when bad news hits, but then looking towards what can be done next and focusing on enjoying what we do have right now. The temptation we face when trials hit is to focus on the trial and become paralyzed with the sadness of it. Thinking back, if that would have been the response of you or any one of us, we would have basically robbed ourselves of five years (and counting!) of awesome opportunities to continue enjoying life together. So that has been a big part of coping . . . allowing myself to grieve and be upset, but also remembering to move forward and intentionally trying to focus on the 'good' that is still right in front of me every day.

The most steadying force in the rollercoaster by far, however, has been having faith in Jesus. You can hit some patches in dealing with a situation like this where it seems like everything just keeps changing or getting worse. Knowing that God's promise of who He is, what He has done, and what He offers us never changes has allowed me to endure all the temporary things that have changed or will change. There have been very rough patches where I've been broken-hearted and very upset in my prayers, but I also think that's where I've grown the most in my faith, because I've found God to be faithful in bringing what my heart needed most at that time. Knowing that there is unchanging hope beyond the mess we face now, as well as providing strength and comfort to face it in the meantime, has been huge for me.

Something that was surprising to me was how long it took me to actually process my own feelings. A year or two into your treatment, a close friend asked how I was doing. I immediately started talking about what was going on with you, what the last scan showed, how you were feeling, etc. My friend interrupted me and said, "No, how are YOU doing?" I realized that while I had probably been asked well over a hundred times about how you were doing, I had never been asked that question before, and I wasn't sure how to answer at first. As we talked, it was helpful to actually put words to what I felt, to grieve how I was unable to do anything to physically take this or change this for my sister, to express my fears, etc. Even though just talking about it wasn't going to change anything, it did help to actually name what was going on inside me, rather than just dealing with a cloud of emotion that had no real definition to it. It's like if I could name it, I could deal with it. Being able to pinpoint some of those feelings helped me to offer them up to God a little easier.

Of course there is also my brother, Eric. A month before my Stage IV diagnosis, my brother met his wife, and for him, she helps him process and survive my diagnosis. Here are his words:

Christy has been a big support for me, talking through things. I've often felt I don't want to bring other family members down with my own fears and sadness, especially you. Christy has been there to give me comfort and support without reminding everyone of the ugly truth.

The other thing that has helped is learning more about it. It doesn't lessen the reality of what it means, but I would rather understand how things work, even if I can't change them. There likely isn't much I can do to help medically, but knowing can help me best direct my efforts to help.

Christy had a unique perspective—meeting the family in one of our most emotionally chaotic times. When I asked her about her experience, she wrote this:

I was nervous about how sensitive the topic of your cancer and treatment was because I didn't really know how the family was handling it or how to ask about it to gain any sort of information. Eric and I had only been dating about two weeks when he mentioned your blog to me, and that was really the first time it came up. So, I spent a whole night reading every single entry so I could be as "up to speed" as possible without having to feel nervous asking, since the relationship was still so new.

After that, I felt like I knew a lot more about the history and your journey, so it eliminated a lot of the general questions I had. From then on it was just a matter of getting to know the family and what to ask and what not to ask. For instance, I remember back when you were not sending us text updates because you didn't receive responses. That was not on purpose, but that was at a time when the results seemed to be constantly negative, and I didn't know what to say. Then, when I realized that I could just respond, "that sucks" I felt like I could send a response. All I wanted to say, was "that sucks" because I didn't know what to say but I wasn't sure how that would be received. I really walked on eggshells about all of it in the beginning because it was a hard thing to come into and not know the people very well and not know what was going on since I hadn't been exposed to cancer so closely before.

So, my advice to others would be to feel it out slowly until you find where your place is. Try to learn as much as you can about it. I didn't feel comfortable just asking the questions out loud, so I learned from reading the blog and doing some research about the disease in general.

In many ways, I think my diagnosis is much harder on my family than it is on me, as they watch me navigate through each scan and treatment decision. And while my family has given me many gifts–laughter, memories, and support—the biggest gift I can give them is permission, the ultimate gift of permission to go on *loving*, *laughing*, and *living* despite grieving. I have told my family and numerous friends diagnosed with cancer to put a time limit on grieving. Honor those deep, dark feelings and get them out. But, set the clock for thirty minutes, then when the time is up, it's time to focus on the next moment rather than let cancer steal any more moments. I trust my family will keep my memory present in the day-to-day of their lives. Their love, no matter how they express it, will continue motivating others profoundly.

"His answer shows that he doesn't see cancer as something *scary*; he is *bravely* at peace with me and the cancer inside of me."

MOTHERING

I have to take a deep breath and admit I'm so terrified to write this, not because I doubt my mothering skills, but because I'm not sure that words can capture the vast, absolute love I have for Corbin. I'm not sure it's possible to translate the infinite love I have for my son to mere words on a page. The black font is so precise against the white page; a sharp contrast to the unending, eternal, immense love I have for my son.

Some Stage IV cancer patients choose to purchase cards and gifts for their children's future events they know they won't see. Holidays, birthdays, graduations, weddings, grandchildren, etc. They hope to have a presence, even though cancer has stolen them from that milestone moment. When Corbin was the ring bearer for my brother's wedding, and I pinned a flower on his lapel, I said a prayer—begging to be able to pin a flower on his tux when he is the groom one day. The same magical moment happened four years later as I pinned a flower on his tux as a ring bearer for my sister's wedding. And I said the same prayers—begging to be able to see him as a groom. As desperately as I want to, I am not so sure I will have the chance. But I have not purchased cards or presents for Corbin's future. I haven't been able to videotape myself in a monologue trying to express a love that knows no bounds.

When I was initially diagnosed Stage IV, I bought a little journal at the local bookstore. The front of the journal was decorated with bright splashes of color, and real flowers were pressed into it. I started writing to Corbin and have named it *Just In Case*. Just in case I'm not here, these are the things I want him to know.

The first entry was written on November 3, 2008: The day after his second birthday, and on that day I wrote about the purpose of the journal and my extreme love for him. I don't have a set schedule for when or what I write to him. I've written funny words he's said such as "ni-ross-or-ris" for rhinoceros. I've written about what traits I hope he looks for in his spouse. I've written about the importance of having integrity in all aspects of his life. I've traced his handprint inside of mine. I've written about how we are alike, having the same golden-brown colored eyes and how we both get crabby when we are hungry or tired. I've also written about how we're different: how Corbin always finds a way to sleep on top of the covers no matter how many times I cover him up; whereas I can't sleep without at least a sheet covering me. I have also included favorite quotes and poems that express how I feel

toward my son. The following, by an unknown author, articulates
the huge, endless love I have for Corbin:

I am here.

I am deep in your heart.

I am in all the joys we lived together, all the sorrows too.

I am in the way you walk and talk and smile.

I am in the things I taught you that you don't even remember learning.

I am in the sunshine of your day, the rain and the storm clouds too.

I am in your talent and your treasures, deep inside.

I am in the look in your eyes when you wonder and behold the day.

I am in your tears that search for me and cannot see for the rain
within your eyes.

I am in your longing to find me once more close to you.

Here I am, wherever you may be. There I am, wherever you go.

Carry me within you as I once carried you.

Deep inside where no one, nothing can ever take me from you.

Be at peace, my beloved child.

Mom is here.

And as much as I want to shelter Corbin from the brutal
reality of cancer, I can't. So instead I try to pour all my love into
him in hope it will sustain him in the future. I also strive to pass
along the values, knowledge, and faith that will allow him to not
only survive but thrive.

Impressively, Corbin has proven that he can thrive through
hardship. It was just at his nine month-old check-up that I said to

his pediatrician, "I found a lump." And while she assured me it was probably nothing, she urged me to get it checked out. When I was diagnosed, I called to thank her for recommending I have it checked out. She said, "I have another young mom in my practice who has breast cancer, and she has always said she would be willing to talk to someone else diagnosed." I gave the pediatrician permission to pass along my information to the other mother, Maria. A mother of two toddlers, she and I quickly connected. We had play dates and enjoyed our time together. Maria started developing back pain a month after a clean scan and when the persistent pain didn't go away, the doctors discovered cancer throughout her entire body. The pain was so intense that Maria was hospitalized. I saw Maria, one day when I was at chemo, and although she was on substantial pain killers, she said, "When I get out of here, I want us to take the kids and play . . . forget about cancer and just be *moms*." I agreed and promised when she was out of the hospital, we could have a play date. Maria, though, remained hospitalized, and several weeks later, she died. We never had that play date.

Since her death over four years ago, I've kept in touch with her widowed husband, Todd, and kept my commitment to Maria to have play dates with our children. In doing so, I have witnessed the resilience of Maria's children, and this is comforting: Knowing that someday Corbin will learn he is not the only one who has a mommy in Heaven.

Maybe the tremendous pain at the thought of not being in his life is because of the tremendous effort required in creating his life. Corbin wasn't a "whoops," "surprise," or "let's see what happens." Corbin's life was created very intentionally.

While trying to get pregnant, I researched and did what I could do to help with the process. I charted my temperature every single morning before getting out of bed because when your temperature rises, ever so slightly, it indicates that ovulation has occurred. After a year of unsuccessful attempts to get pregnant, my former husband and I visited a fertility specialist. After running a myriad of tests, the doctor informed us that I had Polycystic Ovarian Syndrome. A simple explanation: My ovaries had eggs, but my body didn't reach a hormone surge to release the egg for ovulation and potential pregnancy. This is a common infertility diagnosis, so the doctor was optimistic that the IUI procedure would work and achieve pregnancy. The procedure started weeks before the insemination, I had to start the cycle by taking a drug to suppress my ovaries. For five days I took the drug, Femara, to keep my ovaries suppressed. Ironically, this drug is often used as an anti-estrogen treatment in women with breast cancer; for me it offered the same benefit, keeping my ovaries suppressed until it was time to stimulate them to grow an egg. I had to self-inject levels of hormones to stimulate my ovaries. Every evening, I would retreat to my bedroom to give myself a shot in my stomach to signal to my ovaries to grow an egg. Along with this came routine blood work to check my hormone levels. Once they reached the desired range, I had to inject the "trigger" shot. This shot of hormones would trigger my ovaries to release the egg. The trigger shot was timed precisely for thirty-six hours before the insemination. And then the wait. We had to wait for two weeks before more blood work would confirm if I was pregnant.

I vividly remember sitting in the waiting room that housed both infertility patients and regular obstetrics and gynecology. As I sat in my chair and surveyed the other people in the waiting room, I saw a young girl, clearly in her teens with a belly protruding beneath her shirt. In high school health class, we were lectured about using protection to keep from getting pregnant. Now, as an adult, at a time in my life where I felt I could bring a child into the world, my body wouldn't cooperate. At another visit, I heard the patient before I saw her. In walked an inmate from the local jail, shackled, but at the clinic for prenatal care. I was desperate to start a family and knew that time was against me and the window of motherhood was closing. At the same time, many of my friends from college were getting pregnant without even trying. So when I went through infertility treatment, I felt like pregnant women were everywhere stalking me. Even though I've lost my hair twice due to chemotherapy treatments; I've never felt like women having a "good hair day" were stalking me.

I was ecstatic when we got pregnant on the first cycle of infertility treatments. I would be a mother, at last. Excitedly, we attended the first ultrasound. As I lay on the table watching images appear on the monitor, we learned there was a sac for the embryo, but no heartbeat. I was devastated; the vision of motherhood disappeared. My own heart struggled to beat after seeing the embryo inside me didn't have a heartbeat. Since I was an infertility patient, I chose to have genetic testing completed on the tissue they collected from the embryo. They were able to explain why the embryo ceased developing; a chromosome abnormality. They were also able to tell me the chromosomes showed the embryo was male. While I am so very grateful to have successfully delivered Corbin, my six-year-old, I feel at peace knowing I will one day meet the son I was never able to deliver.

And oddly enough, I think my infertility diagnosis actually prepared me in some ways for my breast cancer diagnosis. Both, for example, require frequent doctor's appointments and blood work. For infertility, they closely monitored my hormone levels; for oncology, they monitor my tumor marker levels. For both types of appointments, I often felt out of place. At the time I was going through infertility treatment, I had to wait in the same area as obstetrics and gynecology. I sat in the waiting room, envious of the other patients with a protruding stomach. At the cancer center, I sit in the waiting room filled with people who are decades older than I am. I desperately want to grow old, but can't relate to the elderly cancer patients who have watched their children grow and met their grandchildren. Additionally, there are extensive medications required with each. To get the ovaries to function and grow an egg, I had to give myself daily injections of hormones, and then a precisely timed "trigger" shot to release the egg exactly 36 hours before the procedure. Now, as a cancer patient, I give myself daily shots for three days following chemotherapy to help stimulate white blood cell production to help boost my immune system. While blood work, and ultimately an ultrasound, would reveal if I was successfully pregnant, blood work and a scan shows if there is progression or if the cancer treatment is successful and the cancer is stable. For a very long time, my body has been a clinical item: Something poked, tested, and studied to reveal if the respective goal is achieved. Between infertility and breast cancer, all physical modesty has been stripped from me. And I also learned that I can't trust my body. It failed at my attempts to get pregnant without intervention. It has also turned against me as the cancer has developed, mutated, and grown resistant to chemotherapy treatment.

And, in the time since my Stage IV diagnosis, I've become very intentional about what I share and how I spend time with my son. It began the first Mother's Day after that terminal diagnosis. I had a sense of urgency to take my son on a memorable vacation since no one could predict how long I would have left. We spent five days in Orlando, Florida. While at Disney World, I heard Corbin's deep belly laugh and squeals of sheer glee as we went on rides. While exploring the theme park and hearing his pure elation, I made a promise to myself: as long as I'm able, each year for

Mother's Day, I will take Corbin to a different amusement park. It would be a unique tradition, but one we could enjoy through adventure, fun, and laughter. The best gift Corbin can give me is allowing me entrance into his world, exploring it from his level. Since my original promise to myself at Disney World in 2009, we've also gone to Six Flags St. Louis, Six Flags Over Texas, and Disney Land in California. Each trip has strengthened our bond while making memories. My hope is that my family will continue this tradition with Corbin when I'm no longer here to make those trips and memories with him.

I also hope that these memories will continue and eventually sustain Corbin. He knows I have cancer, but he doesn't understand cancer is what will ultimately take my life. I'm comforted in knowing that cancer isn't a big, ugly, scary word for him. He has only known a mommy with cancer. Recently we were filling out a book, *All About Mommy and Me*. This book has writing prompts to fill in and quizzes to answer about each of us. While completing a quiz about how well we know one another, we came to the question: What do each of us collect? My answer about Corbin was easy: He collects Legos. When he answered the question about what I collect, he said, "Cancer." I laughed and said, "What do you mean by that, buddy?" He logically answered, "Well, you keep getting it, so it's like you collect it." What a practical, rational answer for a six-year-old. While I laughed and agreed with his rationale, inside my heart broke. In his mind, "collecting cancer" was a benign hobby, not a terminal disease. But a friend reminded me that his answer shows that he doesn't see cancer as something scary; he is bravely at peace with me and the cancer inside of me.

Since I have an advanced warning of my death, I have tried to teach Corbin about mortality in general. While our society generally shuns this topic, I've tried to explain that death is a normal process of life. The truth is: We will all die someday—we just don't know when. I also realize that I am highly sensitive to how Corbin reacts to death. When our elderly dog, Guinness, recently died, I tried to help facilitate a healthy mourning process. In some ways, I used Guinness's death as a trial run, of sorts, for my own. In hopes of giving him comfort, I told him that every time we found one of Guinness's hairs (and she left plenty behind), it meant she was wagging her tail in Heaven and thinking of us. This has comforted him, and we frequently talk about Guinness and the others we know in Heaven.

I've also tried to anticipate how things will play out after my death. When Corbin started kindergarten this fall, I scheduled a meeting with his principal. I asked: "If something happens to me during the school year, is Corbin able to stay in school here since his father, who lives in a nearby town, will gain custody?" The principal, shocked at my question, had tears in her eyes and replied, "You don't plan on dying, do you?" I replied, "I don't plan on dying, but I also didn't plan on having Stage IV breast cancer." My reality was deeply upsetting to her. She took a moment to compose herself then stated that residency verification is only done at the beginning of each school year, and as long as Corbin's father would transport him to school, he could finish out the school year at his current school. While the conversation may have been shocking and upsetting for the principal, it gave me a sense of peace knowing that if I die during the school year, Corbin can remain in a familiar environment while grieving and adjusting to my absence. I trust that Corbin's father will honor this wish—as I know he wants what is best for our beloved son.

While I fear how my death will impact Corbin, I do not fear being replaced. Maybe that is one benefit of being divorced. I have witnessed how Corbin has assimilated into a blended family. Corbin gets to experience what it is like being one of many, with his step-siblings at his father's house. In contrast, he is an only child while at my house, and when people ask if I have other children, I'm able to honestly answer that Corbin is: "My first, last, only, and favorite." While society has stigmatized divorce, Corbin hasn't. Because he was two at the time of the divorce, he doesn't remember his father and I ever being together. Recently, one of Corbin's friends declared herself to be the most awesome person in the world. In response, Corbin countered: "You're not the most awesome. God is. And my mom. And my dad." I am confident that Corbin feels loved and secure.

In the fourth season of the popular TV show *Parenthood*, one of its characters, a young mom, is diagnosed with breast cancer.

And while the show is purely fictional, actress Monica Potter, or Kristina Braverman on the show, absolutely nailed it. I tuned in to be a snarky critic at how a fictional show glamorized the disease. The writers of the show gave the character an authentic and accurate portrayal of being a cancer patient. In one episode, she craves normalcy and goes out dancing with her sisters before acknowledging her reality and shaving her head bald. In another episode, I could relate to Kristina as she was unable to plan for her future. She turned down her husband's surprise vacation because she couldn't see a future beyond her scan that would show if she was in remission. While it is refreshing to see the show "got it," it's also a bit like looking in the mirror. In the Christmas episode, her character made a video for her children that so perfectly captured my own feelings toward Corbin. In the video, Kristina states: "I may not always be with you the way I want to be, but I will never leave your side. I'll always be with you. And I'm so lucky I got to be your mom."

And, when my days of mothering are over and cancer has stolen me from my son, I hope he knows that he is the love of my life, and I am *so lucky* I got to be his mom.

NOTES

CH 1. WRITING

Average life expectancy less than 3 years: Metastatic Breast Cancer Network, "Statistics" http://mbcn.org/education/category/statistics/ (accessed February 6, 2013)

CH 3. FREAKING OUT

Normal white blood cell count over 4500: National Institute of Health, "WBC Count" http://www.nlm.nih.gov/medlineplus/ency/article/003643.htm (accessed March 24, 2013)

CH 4. EDUCATING

Statistically when I should have been dead: Metastatic Breast Cancer Network, "Statistics" http://mbcn.org/education/category/statistics/ (accessed February 6, 2013)

CH 5. PINK-WASHING®

Think Before You Pink®: Breast Cancer Action, "Think Before You Pink" Website: http://thinkbeforeyoupink.org (accessed February 6, 2013)

Eli Lilly Milking Cancer: Breast Cancer Action, "Milking Cancer" Blog: http://thinkbeforeyoupink.org/?page_id=2 (accessed February 6, 2013) rBGH/rBST ban: Gucciardi, Anthony (2012, November 6). Banned in 27 Countries, Monsanto's rBGH Inhabits Many U.S. Dairy Products. Natural Society. Retrieved March 24, 2013, from http://naturalsociety.com/banned-in-27-countries-monsanto-rbgh-dairy-milk-products/

Eli Lilly Profits: Breast Cancer Action, "Milking Cancer" Blog: http://thinkbeforeyoupink.org/?page_id=2 (accessed February 6, 2013)

Parabens and breast cancer: Wiley-Blackwell (2012, January 11). Parabens in breast tissue not limited to women who have used underarm products. ScienceDaily. Retrieved February 6, 2013, from http://www.sciencedaily.com/releases/2012/01/120111223348.htm

Lucy Activewear's response: Blog: http://pinkgoose.wordpress.com/2012/09/07/more-fun-with-pinkwashing/ (accessed February 6, 2013)

Cause marketing: Breast Cancer Action, "Cause Marketing" Blog: http://thinkbeforeyoupink.org/?page_id=36 (accessed February 6, 2013)

History of the pink ribbon: Sandy M. Fernandez, "Pretty In Pink" Blog: http://thinkbeforeyoupink.org/?page_id=26 (accessed February 6, 2013)

Only 2% of funding for Stage IV research: Metavivor: "Awareness" Blog: http://www.metavivor.org/Awareness.html (accessed March 24, 2013)

30% of patients diagnosed will progress to Stage IV: Metastatic Breast Cancer Network, "Statistics" http://mbcn.org/education/category/statistics/ (accessed February 6, 2013)

History of breast cancer organizations: Cancer Resource Center: "History of Breast Cancer Advocacy" http://www.crcfl.net/content/view/history-of-breast-cancer-advocacy.html (accessed March 24, 2013)

CH 6. CONNECTING

Giuliana Rancic's biography: Wikipedia: "Giuliana Rancic" http://en.wikipedia.org/wiki/Giuliana_Rancic (accessed February 6, 2013)

History of Infertility: Wikipedia: "In Vitro Fertilisation" http://en.wikipedia.org/wiki/IVF (accessed February 6, 2013)

History of Lindsay Avner: The Every Girl: "Lindsay Avner of Bright Pink" http://theeverygirl.com/feature/lindsay-avner-of-bright-pink/ (accessed March 25, 2013)

CH 7. GRIEVING

211,000 women diagnosed with breast cancer: Center for Disease Control, "Breast Cancer Statistics" http://www.cdc.gov/cancer/breast/statistics/ (accessed March 25, 2013)

49,000 diagnosed with metastatic breast cancer: Metastatic Breast Cancer Network, "Statistics" http://mbcn.org/education/category/statistics/ (accessed February 6, 2013)

40,000 will die annually: Metastatic Breast Cancer Network, "Statistics" http://mbcn.org/education/category/statistics/ (accessed February 6, 2013)

CH 8. UNDERSTANDING

40,000 women die from the disease annually: Metastatic Breast Cancer Network, "Statistics" http://mbcn.org/education/category/statistics/ (accessed February 6, 2013)

30% will end up Stage IV: Metastatic Breast Cancer Network, "Statistics" http://mbcn.org/education/category/statistics/ (accessed February 6, 2013)

162,000 living with metastatic breast cancer: Metastatic Breast Cancer Network, "Statistics" http://mbcn.org/education/category/statistics/ (accessed February 6, 2013)

MBCN conference: Metastatic Breast Cancer Network, "2012 National Conference, Illinois" http://mbcn.org/special-events/category/2012-national-conference-il/ (accessed March 25, 2013)

CH 9. BELIEVING

Life expectancy less than three years: Metastatic Breast Cancer Network, "Statistics" http://mbcn.org/education/category/statistics/ (accessed February 6, 2013)

CH 11. COPING

Champaign-Urbana history: Wikipedia, "Champaign-Urbana Metropolitan Area" http://en.wikipedia.org/wiki/Champaign%E2%80%93Urbana_metropolitan_area (accessed March 25, 2013)

CH 12. MOTHERING

Femara: Femara, "Aromatase Inhibitors" http://www.femara.com/index.jsp (accessed March 25, 2013)

NBC's Parenthood: *What to my Wondering Eyes*. Parenthood. NBC. 11 December 2012. Television.

JEN'S TOP TEN*

There are many opportunities to support cancer-related organizations and charities. These are my top ten favorite cancer-related charities that don't have million-dollar marketing budgets, so you may not have heard of them. Big corporations have already established their place in *cancerland*; however, they often have little direct impact on a personal level. I can assure you that these charities are making a difference in the lives of individuals. Next time, when thinking of making a donation, please consider these charities.

*Since I live in Big 10 country, yet there are rarely just 10 in our conference, I've followed suit and added an 11th charity.

BREAST CANCER ACTION
http://www.bcaction.org

Advocate for more effective and less toxic breast cancer treatments by shifting the balance of power in the Food and Drug Administration's drug approval process away from the pharmaceutical industry and toward the public interest. Decrease involuntary environmental exposures that put people at risk for breast cancer. Create awareness that it is not just genes, but social injustices—political, economic, and racial inequities—that lead to disparities in breast cancer outcomes.

BRIGHT PINK

http://www.brightpink.org

Bright Pink is the only national non-profit organization focusing on the prevention and early detection of breast and ovarian cancer in young women, while providing support for high-risk individuals.

BREAST CANCER RECOVERY

http://www.bcrecovery.org

All retreats are designed by breast cancer survivors for breast cancer survivors. Breast Cancer Recovery embraces all women with breast cancer including all faiths, ages, races, sexual orientations, and financial resources. Women in all stages are welcome to attend - from the newly diagnosed to women many years in remission. Women ages 20 - 71 have attended a retreat. Solo retreat and Mets retreat available.

CONFERENCE FOR YOUNG WOMEN

http://www.c4yw.org

Each year, at this gathering, you'll get the chance to: Hear updates from leading professionals who have dedicated their lives to caring for young women with breast cancer. Learn about new scientific research and clinical care breakthroughs set to offer meaningful benefits to young women with breast cancer or those at risk of developing it. And network with other survivors - share stories, get advice, and experience the joy of meeting someone who understands.

IMERMAN ANGELS

http://www.imermanangels.org

Imerman Angels provides personalized connections that enable 1-on-1 support among cancer fighters, survivors, and caregivers. All services are free and provided for any type, age, stage of cancer.

MEMORIES OF LOVE

http://www.memoriesoflove.org

We help create lasting and loving memories by sending the entire family for five days to Orlando, Florida, for a fun-filled vacation far removed from mounting medical bills, therapy and hospital visits. Through the generosity of corporate partners and sponsors, we are able to provide tickets to the area's best loved theme parks: Universal Studios/Island of Adventures and SeaWorld, as well as a beautiful room at one of a number of Orlando/Kissimmee Resorts, discount meal vouchers, and financial support for travel and incidentals.

METASTATIC BREAST CANCER NETWORK

http://www.mbcn.org

MBCN is a national, independent, nonprofit, patient advocacy group dedicated to the unique concerns of the women and men living with metastatic breast cancer. We strive to help those living with Stage IV breast cancer be their own best advocate through providing education and information on treatments and coping with the disease.

METAVIVOR

http://wwww.metavivor.org

We are a 501(c)3 non-profit organization run entirely by volunteers, mostly with MBC. We created METAvivor because we believe the following: Support for MBC patients is greatly lacking; Awareness of the disease is appalling low; BC mets research is horrendously under-funded.

PINK DAISY PROJECT

http://www.pinkdaisyproject.org

The Pink Daisy Project is a 501(c)3 organization dedicated to helping young women with breast cancer manage treatment a little easier. PDP provides gift cards for groceries, gas, or housecleaning to help young women undergoing treatment.

STUPID CANCER

http://www.stupidcancer.org

Stupid Cancer is a non-profit organization that empowers young adults affected by cancer through innovative and award-winning programs and services. We are the nation's largest support community for this underserved population and serve as a bullhorn for the young adult cancer movement. Our charter is to ensure that no one goes unaware of the age-appropriate resources they are entitled to so they can get busy living.

YOUNG SURVIVAL COALITION

http://youngsurvival.org

Young Survival Coalition (YSC) is the premier global organization dedicated to the critical issues unique to young women who are diagnosed with breast cancer. YSC offers resources, connections, and outreach so women feel supported, empowered, and hopeful.

ACKNOWLEDGMENTS

My deepest appreciation to the GDS 172 Typography II class at Parkland College for creating the beautiful cover and stunning interior layout. Thank you for your patience as I kept adjusting things to get everything just right. Led by professor Gretchen Wieshuber, the class consisted of: Jonny Ashikyan, Gabe Bridwell, Bissie Buscombe, Gary Cosat, Susan Coulter, Whitney Coulter, Katie Eden, Benji Frazzetto, Ricky Greer, Alisha Kirkley, Justin Klett, Ivan Salazar, Scott Sheltra, and Lisa Williamson.

To my dedicated co-writer, Teri Fuller, editors Karen Morgan and Ann Harshbarger, and proof-reader Anna Mehl. You are all so brilliant, and this book would not exist without you.

To fashion stylist Eric Himel. Without the makeover you provided, the cover would not have been possible.

To the linguistically talented Hon. Colonel Esteban A. Bringas for your support, advice, and dazzling ability to transform words.

To Breast Cancer Action, thank you for your review of Pink-Washing® and additional input towards the chapter.

To my doctors, nurses, and staff at Carle Cancer Center. I know I would not be alive without you and the work you do every day.

To my prayer warriors, you have been essential in keeping me full of love and support even when I didn't think I could keep going.

My genuine gratitude to my close friends who were willing to "go there" and share their emotions. Your perspectives are so unique, yet so powerful in conveying how this disease impacts more than the one diagnosed.

My dedicated, amazing family. Mom, Dad, Eric, Christy, Jaxson, Sara, and Noah. Your love has sustained me during my darkest moments. Your support has helped me enjoy my dazzling moments. Without you, my quality of life would be so poor, it wouldn't be worth continuing. Thank you for sharing your perspectives, each was incredibly distinctive to exactly who you are and I love you for that.

And, to my favorite. Corbin, you are the reason I continue to move forward in life. You are the most precious miracle I ever could have hoped for. I am so fortunate to be your mom, and I will forever love you most.

21892532R00106

Made in the USA
Charleston, SC
03 September 2013